NEVER
ASK FOR
THE SALE

NEVER ASK FOR THE SALE

Supercharge Your Business with the Power of Passionate Ambivalence

SUE HEILBRONNER

balance

New York   Boston

Balance
Hachette Book Group
1290 Avenue of the Americas
New York, NY 10104
GCP-Balance.com
@GCPBalance

First Edition: September 2025

Balance is an imprint of Grand Central Publishing. The Balance name and logo are registered trademarks of Hachette Book Group, Inc.

The publisher is not responsible for websites (or their content) that are not owned by the publisher.

The Hachette Speakers Bureau provides a wide range of authors for speaking events. To find out more, visit hachettespeakersbureau.com or email HachetteSpeakers@hbgusa.com.

Balance books may be purchased in bulk for business, educational, or promotional use. For information, please contact your local bookseller or email the Hachette Book Group Special Markets Department at Special.Markets@hbgusa.com.

Print book interior design by Jeff Stiefel.

Library of Congress Cataloging-in-Publication Data

Name: Heilbronner, Sue author
Title: Never ask for the sale: supercharge your business with the power of passionate ambivalence / Sue Heilbronner.
Description: First edition. | New York: Balance, 2025. | Includes bibliographical references and index.
Identifiers: LCCN 2025005075 | ISBN 9780306836237 hardcover | ISBN 9780306836244 trade paperback | ISBN 9780306836251 ebook
Subjects: LCSH: Success in business | Success | Self-actualization (Psychology)
Classification: LCC HF5386 .H3785 2025 | DDC 650.1—dc23/eng/20250613
LC record available at https://lccn.loc.gov/2025005075

ISBNs: 978-0-306-83623-7 (hardcover); 978-0-306-83625-1 (ebook)

Printed in the United States of America

LSC-C

Printing 1, 2025

For Leah,
the catalyst for and champion of the best in me

CONTENTS

PART 1
USING THIS BOOK

PART 2
CLEARING THE BLOCKERS TO SUCCESS

PART 3
DEFINING THE "YOU" IN YOUR SELLING MOTION

PART 4

LAYING THE GROUNDWORK FOR SELLING

PART 5

MARKETING YOU:
AUTHENTICALLY, IMPERFECTLY, AND OFTEN

PART 6

SELLING YOU: FROM PROSPECT TO CLOSE

FOREWORD

As a lifetime entrepreneur and investor in early-stage startups, I have come to appreciate—in myself and others—the talent and tenacity it takes to move from idea to reality. At the most basic level, selling is required to make that leap, whether selling an actual or planned product, a startup investment opportunity, the vision for a new cultural institution, or a service offered by a solopreneur provider. As I reflect on my own experience building companies and venture firms fueled by technology innovation, I realize that I've always been selling. My selling has not been overt but rather a function of how I expressed something I cared about and was building to bring other people along for the ride.

In *Never Ask for the Sale: Supercharge Your Business with the Power of Passionate Ambivalence*, Sue Heilbronner lays the philosophical and tactical groundwork for this authentic selling, which doesn't express itself as typical sales. *Never Ask* gives readers a path to connect their business pursuits to their greatest skills or talents, which allows selling of any kind to be an outgrowth of personal and professional alignment.

Sue recommends that this holistic approach to growing a business be intimately tied to leveraging community, building genuine relationships, and a notion I helped coin at Techstars, #givefirst, which means you are willing to put energy into a relationship or a system without defining the transactional parameters. However, it's not altruism. You expect to get something back. But you don't know when or from whom, in what form or consideration, or over what time frame.

The crux of *Never Ask* is the selling philosophy Sue calls *passionate ambivalence*. This term seems contradictory but ultimately proves to be a critical component for entrepreneurs and solopreneurs to build sustainable companies.

Sue argues that the best way to sell is to focus less on the close or the outcome. Instead, she encourages sellers of all kinds to be as deeply passionate about a project, engagement, or new business partnership as they are while staying unattached to whether the sale closes. Passionate ambivalence is the optimal outlook for a seller who wants to optimize closing the best deals with the most desirable customers at the best available price point.

Sue's extensive background spans from being a lawyer to being a tech entrepreneur, investor, and well-respected executive coach. As such, she comes to the topic of selling in the broadest sense with great authority and experience. She brings her knowledge and storytelling to *Never Ask* in a vulnerable and engaging way. She also shares stories of entrepreneurs with whom she has worked to add flavor to the actionable lessons of the book. The blend of story and content makes *Never Ask* feel as valuable as a great coaching session with Sue on amplifying your potential in building something about which you care deeply.

Brad Feld
Foundry, Partner
Techstars, cofounder
Aspen, Colorado
July 2024

INTRODUCTION

I have been selling my entire life.

At age five, I loaded up my Radio Flyer with kids' books. I wrote prices in crayon on the covers and ambled around my neighborhood shilling. I don't remember if I sold a thing.

That was just the start.

In my life, I've also sold

- Women's clothes at the Limited store in the mall
- Extremely excellent bagels to fund the debate team at Miami Palmetto Senior High School
- McDonald's children's birthday parties as the designated polyester-clad "birthday lead"
- Godfather's pizza
- The idea of a magical day at Disney World from my perch as a seasonal employee taking tickets at the main gate
- Rides on the Space Spiral and various roller coasters at Cedar Point
- Ice cream in Lincoln City, Oregon, where I got scolded for making my scoops too large
- The value of a lovely stay at Oregon's Salishan Coastal Lodge through my housekeeping services
- Rides to the Cleveland airport from Oberlin College
- Fifteen hamburgers and everything else on the menu of the late Hamburger Hamlet in Washington, DC. I still remember the burgers by number.

- The importance of a tricameral system of government to high school students as an instructor with the Close Up Foundation
- Home goods designed around the TV show *Trading Spaces* and marketed at the late Linens 'n Things
- Dog toys licensed by and created for the television brand Animal Planet at Petco
- On-time subscription delivery for HVAC filters at the self-founded and aptly named OnTimeAirFilters.com
- Philosophies of entrepreneurship as an adjunct graduate school professor at the University of Colorado
- Slots in the MergeLane Fund's startup accelerator focused on companies with at least one woman in leadership
- Internet marketing products and services for independent hotels and large hospitality companies at the late TIG Global (now Micros)
- Software as a service payment processing for small businesses at PaySimple (now EverCommerce)
- Seats at Conscious Leadership Camps, Conscious Leadership Forums, and the Certification for Leader Coaches program

These are just the things I was paid to sell. I have also been a passionate advocate and ad hoc influencer, recommending amazing web designers, copywriters, therapists, dentists, restaurants, Costco finds, and more. Sometimes I've done this so well that when I want to use a service provider again, I suddenly can't get on their schedule—in part because of the demand I have cultivated. I'm good with that. Mostly.

In law school, my favorite classes were related to business. In my eighth year as a lawyer, I founded a baby-products company called Y2Wear—Clothing and Accessories for the Millennium Baby. I struck a few strategic partnerships. I earned some press in the *Chicago Tribune*. I only once made the harrowing gaffe of asking a nonpregnant woman when she was due. I realized that you can't build a business with a one-year time horizon and changed the brand from its new-millennium focus to a more general baby-gift company.

I loved it. What I loved most was the feeling of making a sale. It was exhilarating. It was money in the bank. It was the little rush of energy that comes from knowing that the thing I have is valuable to another person.

I loved it so much that when I compared the dynamism of my little venture to my "dream job" as a criminal prosecutor for the Department of Justice Civil Rights Division, I could feel my energy being pulled from selling stories to juries to selling products to consumers.

I left the practice of law for a job in online business development at Discovery Communications (now Warner Bros. Discovery). A colleague at Discovery bought the baby-products business for $12,500. That covered most of what I'd lost in running it. I considered the entire venture to be an inexpensive MBA.

Ever since, I have been selling full-time. I've been a chief revenue officer or chief executive officer of technology startups. For the last decade, I have been selling myself.

Twelve years ago, when I was a partner at a tech startup, I encountered a body of work called conscious leadership. A coach named Kaley Klemp introduced it to me. Meeting Kaley changed my life. I delved into the principles of conscious leadership. The changes in me were so noticeable that family and friends wanted to learn what I had been up to, and they, too, dove into conscious leadership. Two years after meeting Kaley, I started my own company to do coaching and facilitation with a focus on conscious leadership.

I made this decision aggressively but not fearlessly.

Because the very successful Kaley and her then co-coaches Jim Dethmer and Diana Chapman were my teachers and role models, I knew I could generate a meaningful, sustainable, even wildly successful solopreneur business as an executive coach, speaker, and facilitator. And because I want to serve as a transparent and successful model to others who have worked closely with me (or are discovering me now for the first time), I chose to write this book.

As an independent coach, facilitator, and speaker, I have spent the lion's share of my work time sparking authentic conversations in service of personal growth and satisfaction—for myself and others. The work is edgy, challenging, provocative, emotional, spiritual, and remarkable. At times, I'm amazed that I've created a life that allows me to work largely when I want, with whom I want, and on topics and in contexts in which I'm interested. Some of my success is presumably connected to being pretty good at what I do; however, a large measure of what I've built is tied to how successfully I sell. In the first six years, my solopreneur coaching and facilitation business grew from zero revenue to more than $1 million a year.

My dear friend Leah Pearlman started referring to my style of sales as "Suemanship," which I alternately loved and resisted. She wasn't talking only about the selling of my coaching services; she was referring to all my advocacy—for my favorite ice cream, a new book, a podcast that blew my mind, or a new friend—as Suemanship. My resistance to this word emanated from the self-judgment that I, apparently, was always selling. But it's true about me. I *am* always selling something, and when I recommend something with the level of conviction I bring to bear, other people tend to try out whatever I'm passionate about. At its center, Suemanship is about my recognition and celebration of brilliance, value, humor, delicious flavors, and more. The more I sat with the moniker "Suemanship" and felt how much love Leah had for this part of me, the more I understood how well it fits.

One night, Leah and I were at a dinner party, parked on a couch in a deep and engaging conversation with a pack of shared friends. One of our friends was asking me how he could grow his new coaching side hustle faster.

I suggested a range of tactics that I had consciously or unconsciously been honing for a lifetime. These notions are not things I gleaned merely from my own experiences launching my own businesses. Because I have been an entrepreneur, mentor, leadership coach, investor, and professor of entrepreneurship, they are also lessons I've absorbed through thirty years of watching hundreds of other entrepreneurs and entrepreneurial sellers launch and grow their businesses. So although I was talking about practices deployed in my current business, most of those practices and perspectives come from decades of insights into other people's businesses.

The tactics that were most surprising to him and the group were the ones that seemed counterintuitive. The approach underlying the methods I was explaining is something I have since named "passionate ambivalence." Passionate ambivalence—the methodology that forms the basis of this book—is the balance of being deeply passionate about a new prospective piece of business and, at the same time, being unattached to whether I land it. I told my friends that night that passionate ambivalence is, in my opinion, the secret sauce to how to grow sales with clients you want most at prices you feel great about. I also shared that I think it's a great approach to selling any product, raising venture capital (VC) from investors, marketing yourself for a new job, writing college admissions essays, and landing the romantic partner of your dreams.

As I was energetically throwing down what I suppose sounded like sales wisdom that night, Leah looked at me and said, "*This* is your book." Within five minutes of her comment, we came up with a plan to run a live and virtual workshop on Suemanship and the power of passionate ambivalence.

One week later, twenty-five people attended that first workshop. In preparation, I had drafted what became the outline of this book. I tweaked the title of the workshop to "youmanship" because I believe you are at the heart of every sale you make. If you establish sufficient confidence in and alignment among your greatest strengths, what you love, and your business (or job), you are most likely to be successful because you are less likely to compromise the core aspects of yourself in building your business or selling your work. From the strength of a you-focused mindset, you could cultivate passionate ambivalence organically.

When I pitched the title "youmanship" to publishers, I received the email equivalent of blank stares. Eventually, my agent, editor, and I settled on the title *Never Ask for the Sale* because never asking for a piece of business is an archetypal example of passionate ambivalence as a selling technique. In short, if you want to sell successfully, you *can* be extremely, authentically passionate about earning and doing a piece of work. At the same time, you need to believe and create a perception that you are so good, so hard to attain, and so unattached to whether you "win" a piece of work that you ought not even to ask for the business. You can't *need* the business. You can't be accommodating in your pricing strategy in a way that implies that you don't value yourself or what you do. You can't send an automated flow of persistent emails about how great you are and how ready you are to get busy on a piece of business, because someone amazing wouldn't have time for this. They would be busy doing other work at premium price points. Instead, you passionately argue for why you or your product are the perfect fit, you spell out a few terms, and you wait to see if you hear back.

If your head just tilted in that doglike "What on earth is she proposing?" way, you're definitely keeping up. I believe that growing sales and building a business depends, in many ways, on acting like you are perfectly fine whether or not you make any incremental sale. In holding this mindset of passionate ambivalence, it is critical to understand how you are at the center of your business and everything you sell. If you have aligned your desires; your natural or acquired gifts; and the product, service, or "pitch" you're making, you often can successfully grow your business through passionate ambivalence.

Enough preamble. One woman who attended a recent workshop I gave to help flesh out this book summed up my advice like this:

"Just chill the F out and get going."

So let's do that.

PART 1

USING THIS BOOK

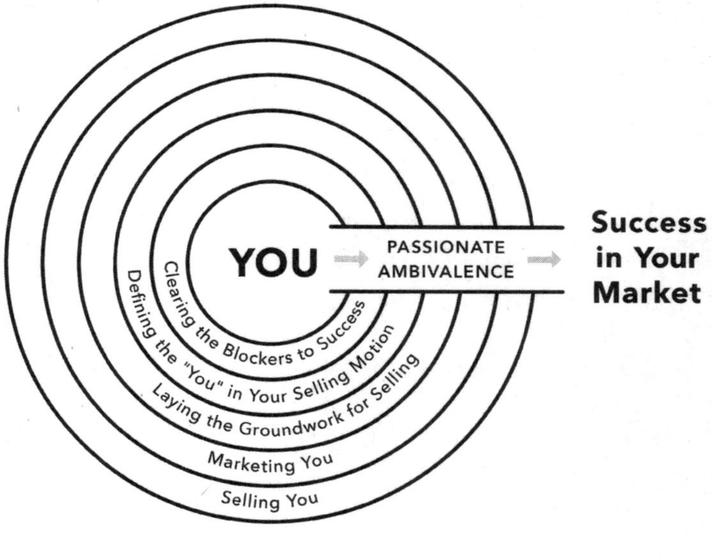
YOU
PASSIONATE
AMBIVALENCE
Success
in Your
Market
Clearing the Blockers to Success
Defining the "You" in Your Selling Motion
Laying the Groundwork for Selling
Marketing You
Selling You

CHAPTER 1

THE AUDIENCE AND STRUCTURE

Selling from the Inside Out

T his book was first conceived with the solopreneur in mind—the entrepreneur who is building a business where they are the primary driver
and where there is little to no intention of hiring employees. There are
more solopreneurs than ever. MBO Partners found that from 2020 to 2022,
the number of independent workers rose by 69 percent, to 21.6 million.[1] I
imagine these figures exclude the number of people managing full-time jobs
and running a business as a side hustle.

The shift to more independent work and solopreneurship is partly associated with the huge social changes wrought by the pandemic and our new
acceptance of remote work. It's partly because of technological changes that
make independent and remote work easier than ever. In the United States,
we can also point to the Affordable Care Act, which means solopreneurs
have much less worry over being stranded without employer-funded health
insurance. I applaud all of this. If solopreneurship is for you, I want you to
be supported in that.

---

1 "The Independent by Choice Movement: Authentic and Intentional: State of Independence
in America 2024," MBO Partners, https://www.mbopartners.com/state-of-independence/.

But solopreneurs are not the only ones who sell, obviously. They're not even the only ones who sell based on the uniqueness that is them. I sold this way during my legal career and again in my corporate career.

When I was working as a federal prosecutor "selling" civil rights cases to a judge or jury, I was the one standing before the court representing the government. My conviction around the rule of law, my preparation for the task at hand, my ability to speak eloquently, my gift for improvisation when needed, and my smarts were all integral to that representation. The facts of the case and the presentations of my witnesses mattered, of course, but there would be no way to take my role out of the mix.

The same is true in selling Internet marketing services. When I told Hyatt in the early 2000s that our company could create more, higher-profit bookings for them directly through the corporate site compared to lower-margin online travel sites, I was part of that message. For me to make that sale, Hyatt needed to know that I (as a representative of our company) understood their wants, their challenges, and their opportunities.

The concepts and tactics in *Never Ask for the Sale* will help you no matter what kind of selling you do, no matter your business context. And it is important to recognize that running a small business focused on marketing your strengths is not mandatory, perfect, easy, or sexy. As you read this resource and others, keep asking yourself whether being a solopreneur or any kind of entrepreneur is the best fit for you. I'm assuming that this is not your only option, and for many people, the relative stability of a steady income and company-provided benefits is quite appealing, especially at times of rapid change (e.g., having a baby, sending your kid to college, caring for aging parents, or navigating divorce).

There's no special merit to taking an independent path. I don't judge it as better than anything else. If you do take it (or continue it), do it with clear intention.

THE STRUCTURE

The structure of this book resembles a set of concentric circles with you at the center. The path crossing these circles from you to the market you're addressing is the strategy and mindset of passionate ambivalence.

This book begins with theories on selling and self-investigation, and it drives toward concrete tactics for selling and marketing a business that depends primarily on you. Interwoven throughout, you'll find anecdotes about my sales experience and stories of other entrepreneurs who have built businesses with, in my estimation, the principles of passionate ambivalence at the center. I suggest you garner insights from those stories and apply them to your own business or sales journey for your maximum learning and application.

YOU AT THE CENTER

To develop your mindset of passionate ambivalence, you must first develop confidence, self-awareness, and alignment between you and the work you're doing. The key to growing your revenue or your sales is to know yourself well enough that you can craft a successful business focused on products or activities you love at price points that are rewarding. As such, at the most fundamental level, this book is a highly practical guide to how to sell *you*—regardless of what you're actually selling—using passionate ambivalence. You'll learn more about what I mean by that later. For now, suffice it to say that selling yourself starts as an inside job.

In this part of the book, I begin with a deep dive into the you that you are selling, and I offer strategies and tactics to complement that awareness. I also address getting to know how you can be successful in a solopreneur business, a service offering that depends heavily on you, or a sales effort in which you are a critical component (I suggest that's true of all sales efforts).

CLEARING THE BLOCKERS TO SUCCESS

Beginning the inside job of looking at yourself as the center of your business growth is a bit of a leap for some. This book will walk you through the steps, tools, and exercises to help you take that leap with conviction. Loving your business idea or the service you have to offer or the work you do is great. On its own, however, that won't get you where you need to be. Selling is all about mindset, which means you must look inside yourself to understand any mental barriers you might have to becoming an amazing seller. This book will help you uncover, face, and address your unconscious commitments, limiting beliefs, and upper limits that may prevent you from achieving your goals for business success. You'll find those strategies and tools in Part 2.

DEFINING THE "YOU" IN YOUR SELLING MOTION

After you've cleared your blockers, you need to start defining yourself—and, by extension, your product or service—in a consistent way. In doing so, you will be creating the foundation for a compelling brand for yourself and your business. When you've done all that, you will be fully ready to experience marketing and sales as an awakening, exhilarating, brilliantly conscious activity, which, not incidentally, is a very important key to your business success. We'll do this work on aligning your gifts with your offering, your two-minute bio, your zone of genius, and goal setting in Part 3.

LAYING THE GROUNDWORK FOR SELLING

Once you have developed a heightened sense of alignment between you, your strengths, and your business offerings, Part 4 will offer you ideas and tactics for laying the early groundwork for your marketing and sales efforts. This is where you will begin making specific connections between who you are and how you can operate as your authentic self in the market.

MARKETING YOU

With the groundwork in place, Part 5 will give you strategic and tactical methods for getting you and your business offering out in the market. I will cover creating your digital and brand presence, launching your online outreach efforts, building visibility in your community and across your network, and creating referral relationships. These are broadcast tools that are critical for attracting the right clientele and priming them to engage with you as a potential solution for their needs.

SELLING YOU

Once you have placed all the scaffolding around yourself, your business, your brand, and your network, it's time for a deep dive into the topic of actually selling. It is here that you will see the myriad ways I believe a mindset of passionate ambivalence and correlated tactics will fuel your success.

In every part of this journey, I will be sharing fully authentic versions of how I leverage passionate ambivalence for these various components of business building. I will be direct, transparent, and at times vulnerable so that you will gain a genuine sense of the highs and lows of my journey in order to apply them to the journey that works for you. Most chapters will include at least one exercise so that you can use this book as a sales "workbook" or "coaching session," building your concentric circles as this book covers them.

I am very aware that some of you do not love selling in the way that I do (yet!). You may have picked up this book *because* you feel a need to sell better but have an aversion to the process. You want to do this better, and there are bonus points if you learn it in a way that feels effortless and authentic. If your resistance is crowding out your "I can do this" voice, I welcome all of that. Even if you do not love selling now, even if you do not love selling by the end of this book, this book is for you.

This book should feel like coaching. My primary role in life and career is to be a coach. I have designed this book to feel like a coaching session with and for you. The provocations and exercises are designed for you to learn more about yourself in service of creating a highly aligned and successful business. I encourage you to play along. Do the exercises; engage with people who love you around the prompts I provide. That will be key to your incorporating the concepts of this book into your own life and career. As I do with all my 1:1 clients, I hope I will challenge you, primarily to reach the greatest possible vision of you. I hope you receive any challenges as invitations to own your full power and your many gifts.

You will learn things about yourself that advance your goals in diverse areas of your life. You will know yourself better. You will articulate your points of view more clearly. You will become more aligned in your life, bringing what you love and what you do into greater harmony. And maybe, just maybe, you'll end up liking sales more.

CHAPTER 2

KNOW BEFORE YOU GO

know you want to start selling. I want you to, too. But please do not skip this chapter.

I don't want this book to set you up for anything other than big success. To ensure that success is the most likely outcome, I'll invite you to be aware of some guideposts before you spend a few hours of your valuable time honing your knowledge and skills.

GUIDEPOST 1

This book is one opinion. It isn't "right" or "true."

When you're reading, you might observe that my tone is steadfast (read: righteous) and absolute.

That said, I'm not arbitrarily righteous and absolute; I have strong views that are informed by deep experience and a mental model that I've tested and retested through engagement with others.

Everything in this book is my opinion refined by other people's feedback. But I am regularly wrong. Although you should take my opinion with a grain of salt, I hope you'll find that there is enough in my background or in what I share in this book that you, like many who have heard this material in my workshops, feel there's real merit to this approach and these tactics.

Even so, I want you to make this book yours, filtering for what makes sense in your business, what resonates, and what you want to discard. The only "right" thing in this book is what is right for you.

One superb example of my conviction is the title of this book, *Never Ask for the Sale*. Please know that when I say "never," I mean "almost never." The title and principles here are guidelines, not absolutes. I have taught these principles enough to know that light bulbs will probably happen. Those are the concepts you should take away. Even if you leave others, I believe you'll end up winning.

GUIDEPOST 2

Generalizations will be made.

I will generalize in this book. As a person who has been a lawyer, entrepreneur, big-company operator, CEO, venture capitalist, and executive coach, I have formed a range of opinions grounded in my experience. I do quite a bit of pattern matching across my time and experiences. At times, you will disagree with me or think my generalizations miss the mark. You will likely be right about that.

GUIDEPOST 3

Everything in this book is selling.

I've already been selling, and I won't stop. I'm endeavoring to be direct, conversational, occasionally amusing, casual, self-deprecating, and a tad audacious. That is precisely how I sell myself. You will have a different approach to selling yourself, and that's wonderful. Just listen to how, in seemingly invisible (dare I say ambivalent) ways, I'm making a case about the value of this content and my credibility to share it. The invisible ways will become more visible as you learn more about my selling philosophy. I've told you a bit about who I am and what I've done, and this very chapter is telling you essentially what I'd like you to sign up for as you read this book. Straddling the fence of wanting you to want to read more and being okay with your decision to stop (i.e., choosing not to sign up to work with me) is at the heart of passionate ambivalence, my guiding selling strategy. You've witnessed this already. Yes, it's a fair warning. But it's also a signal to you about how I sell by not selling.

This form of detached selling is the water I swim in. I can't always see when I'm doing it because it's the general pattern of my being. When you can find *your* natural, *invisible selling motion* and bring it forward, selling yourself will become easier and more conscious.

GUIDEPOST 4

I care about making money in business. If you do not, this book may challenge you (which may not be all bad).

A significant motivator for me in running a business is making money. I like making money for the sake of all the normal things: paying my mortgage, traveling, picking up checks at some group dinners, not having to worry too much about prices at the grocery store, helping my nieces out with college tuition. I also care about it as a decent scoreboard for how well I and my company are doing. I am competitive. I like putting up good numbers. I keep track. I compare this year to previous years. I set goals. Monetary success is not my *only* or even a *primary* value, but I care about it.

Not everyone running a business or engaged in selling cares about making money as much as I do. You may be running an "impact business" by *choice* (as opposed to just having subpar revenue). You may be leading a nonprofit (though fundraising is just selling). Come into the tent.

Now, if you say you care about financial success in your business *and* you have a scarcity mindset about money, this book may challenge you. By a "scarcity mindset," I mean that you don't believe it's possible for you to have enough money or to be financially comfortable. A scarcity mindset may appear in the form of not thinking your work is good enough to warrant clients paying you at rates that allow you to live well.

I believe your beliefs about financial scarcity are fluid, not fixed. First, I'd like you to become aware of any of your beliefs about money that seem limiting. Second, I'd like you to welcome all those beliefs, noticing that they come from a place that makes sense (family upbringing, traumatic past work experience, etc.). Third, I'd like you to wonder how your scarcity beliefs may serve you, either consciously or unconsciously. Perhaps they make you more careful, enabling you to save up for meaningful things without leaking cash on fast fashion or espresso martinis. Perhaps you have known wealthy people whom you've regarded as unkind or worse. As you get to know this part of yourself, see if you can notice that at least *some* of your mindset about money is a matter of choice. If you can get to that level of awareness, you can welcome both the learning and the skepticism you may bring to this book. Then you can hold your historical relationship to money just a bit more loosely, opening the door to what's possible.

GUIDEPOST 5

This book applies to every type of seller (or human).

This book targets primarily solopreneurs (which I define as an entrepreneur who is running a business where they are the driver of success and likely the only full-time employee) whose business involves selling themselves or something comparably intangible.

But if you are selling something else, in a different context, this book is also for you. If you are pursuing any kind of career where you want to put yourself on a positive trajectory, this book is for you. You are selling yourself at every interview, presentation, keynote speech, first date, and holiday party. So much of selling is about selling *you*, regardless of what you think you're selling.

You will also find value here if you are a

+ High school student who wants to increase your chances of identifying and being admitted to the college that is a perfect fit
+ College graduate embarking upon your first job
+ Person starting a new career

- Midcareer professional who wants to reach the next level within your organization
- Professional wanting to pivot to something new in order to make a material jump in your career level
- Lawyer, accountant, architect, home builder, consultant, real estate agent, or any other professional who wants to make some rain inside your company so that you stand a better chance of making partner
- Entrepreneur preparing to market your new idea to investors or to sell your very new product

GUIDEPOST 6

This book works best for people who are superb.

If you are engaged in or contemplating a business where you are the primary product (coaching, consulting, advising, and more), you must be awesome at what you do. This book will be less useful to you if you are average. This book might actually be harmful if you are average.

It doesn't matter what you do. If you are a birthday-party clown, you need to be one of the best birthday clowns in Des Moines. How do you know you're an awesome clown? First, people to whom you're not related say so. Second, you get word-of-mouth inquiries. Third, you have those really giant shoes. That's imperative.

Even if you aren't yet superb at what you're trying to do in your business, ask yourself whether you are superb in general. Are you magnetic? Are you dynamic? Are you extremely thoughtful? Are you able to develop meaningful connections with people (loudly or quietly) in social settings or at work? Do you glean insights that few people see because of the quality of your listening? If you're not sure, think about what people—who are not your family—say about you. Do people seek you out for something? Do they speak glowingly to others about you in introductory emails? Do you have a pattern of excellence in your background, showing numerous accomplishments in open playing fields?

If the answer to most of these questions is no, I recommend considering some of the lessons in this book aspirational for your future awesome self. The daring, contrarian features of *Never Ask for the Sale* depend on your being awesome at most of what you do and in the ways you show up in the world. I will invite you to be very clear about what you're amazing at, to take only work that aligns well with those things, and to turn down work that doesn't meet your revenue objectives. Why? Because work that does meet your objectives will replace it. I will advise that if you put yourself out in the world in the thousands of ways you can, your and your business's flywheel will be operating 24-7, generating eventual high-quality work for you. The first advice I give to all young people coming out of college and attempting to build quality networks is to be awesome at anything they do. People notice. People talk. If you haven't yet experienced the cumulative raising of your boat as an outgrowth of your known awesomeness, I assure you that this book will have lessons to which you will aspire after doing some awesome legwork. If you're just being falsely humble or if your imposter voice is answering this question, you'll be fine.

If you are not superb (yet), some of the ideas in this book could be perilous. They will hang you out to dry, having already invested in building the foundation of a you-focused business. You will come across as arrogant instead of solid, as crazy in your pricing rather than offering a premium product. Instead of reading *Never Ask for the Sale*, choose a less aggressive and more process- and funnel-driven approach to selling.

If we're good on this front—if you can find the awesome and superb inside you—let's keep moving down the road.

GUIDEPOST 7

Even if you are superb, sometimes things go south.

You can be extraordinary, and you can do everything in this book and the other six books you read on building a business before you found this one, and there will still be hard days. I don't lose much business that I really want, but I lose some. Even if I'm able to reach the level of passionate ambivalence, a few of those losses sting.

In addition, when you do make a great sale and grow a piece of business in a way that meets your and your clients' desires, clients do not last forever. Whether due to macroeconomic conditions, a perceived misstep in the work, or a personal misalignment that emerges over time, you will lose long-term business. Perhaps you won't, but I have.

I recently lost a five-year piece of work. There were a few factors that caused this, but the essence is simple. I came into the company as a facilitator for a two-day off-site, and that relationship grew into what I call a company coaching role, where I participate in all executive team meetings, coach the executives, facilitate all executive team off-sites, and do other useful things that arise during the relationship. In year five, the CEO—by then a dear friend and astonishing ally in my business—started saying that he thinks most coaches have "one or two tricks." He said it playfully, but the comment began to grind me. That likely meant there was truth in what he was saying, but I had the story that I'd done *so much* with this company over the years during many different times in its life. The CEO had told me I was partly responsible for the retention of key leaders. And then, one day in the middle of a one-year agreement for me to serve in the company coach role, he told me he wanted exposure to a different style and approach. That meant I would no longer be the executive team coach. He asked if we could end the relationship with a reasonable monetary accommodation. I took a few hours to process the emotions and shed the tears, then went back to him and said of course.

The only thing better than doing great work is seeing that fact evidenced in growing the piece of work or getting word-of-mouth referrals that spin out of that work. And sometimes, when you put yourself out there as a solopreneur (or any kind of person who sells), things turn the other way. My goal has been to hold a wide perspective about those less-than-delightful moments and to complete those relationships mindfully. I recently had dinner with the executive team of the company I just mentioned. I told them that it was their decision to cut me loose that gave me the impetus and a bit of time to write this book. For me, these things have a way of working out.

GUIDEPOST 8

Feel any emotions that arise if you want to.

This is an invitation. Even with these guiding principles in mind, this book may make you mad. It might also prompt other emotions like sadness or fear. I will challenge how you talk about yourself and your products. I will cast aspersions on your pricing scheme. I will suggest that your nice-guy-deferential-likable persona may win you lots of friends but fewer premium customers. I absolutely hope some of this feels relatable, personal, and perhaps even confrontational. Keen. I think anger and fear are reliable catalysts for change. I also believe that feeling emotions is valuable as an end in itself. Plus, you might feel pure delight in having some new tools and mindsets to apply to growing your business, and that emotion is especially welcome.

CHAPTER 3

SELLING YOURSELF VERSUS SELLING ANOTHER PRODUCT

When I first embarked on my journey of selling my own coaching and consulting services, I often got stuck on what felt like the unique experience of selling myself versus some other, more concrete product. I've had successful sellers tell me that they love selling in general, but selling themselves feels more threatening. They say the risk of getting a no feels like a far more personal rejection.

I wholly reject the story that selling yourself is harder. You know the product better than anything else, after all. So let's dig into the differences and the ways to get comfortable with the idea of selling yourself.

Every one of my early sales roles involved selling something that felt distinct from me, but in the most recent chapter of my career, I transitioned to making myself part of the product. I cofounded a VC fund, MergeLane, with a local friend and startup angel investor, Elizabeth Kraus. For years, we ran a startup accelerator, a three-month boot-camp program for founders where we provided education and mentorship in exchange for 6 percent of the equity in the participating startup companies. Ultimately, the Merge-Lane Fund raised more than $7 million and over a ten-year span invested in fifty-four startups, including many that had successful exits. MergeLane was one of the first venture funds with a quasi–impact lens, and I was proud to put my time, heart, and money where my beliefs were. That said, we viewed the fund—correctly, as it turned out—as the "smart" rather than the "right" thing to do. A key part of the MergeLane programs was selling start-ups on the value of our coaching, mentor and investor network, and advice in exchange for equity in their early-stage companies.

Similarly, in my current roles as an executive coach, facilitator, speaker, advisor, speaker trainer, program leader, and now author, I am constantly marketing the value I bring to these assignments. It's personal. It's intimate. It's vulnerable. That's what I *love and sometimes fear* about it.

I have owned the idea of selling myself so much that I now market all my offerings under the domain name HeySue.com. I started with a more generic domain, which remains my corporate entity name: Boulder Ideas. Then I decided to step into the notion that I am selling myself, and I pivoted to SueHeilbronner.com. And *then*, in an act of pure late-night daring, I was able to jettison my cumbersome last name and own the idea that what I am selling is, often, "Sue."

This is an extreme example of owning the idea of selling yourself. But you get the picture. When you are selling yourself, you don't have the option of pivoting to a different product. You are pretty much stuck with you.

I see examples of people selling themselves in most business contexts. My lens may be a bit colored, but if you try on these glasses with a few of my examples, you might gain an appreciation of how to leverage this point of view for your own selling efforts. My two examples come in radically different markets: preloved apparel and AI coding tools for developers.

AN EXAMPLE:
PUTTING ONESELF AT THE CENTER OF RETAIL SELLING

Margaret Miner founded a high-end consignment store called Rags Consignments in Boulder, Colorado, in 1995. Rags prides itself on its excellent curation of incoming inventory—women's clothing and accessories. The merchandise is current, clean, and high-quality. The consignment model allows people to submit their used clothing for review by the selective curators at Rags. If clothes are accepted, they hit the floor, and the consignors and Rags split the revenue from any sold item.

Margaret opened Rags after years of holding preloved clothing sales in the basement of her home. She curated the collection, invited friends over, and used her not-insubstantial styling talent to make people look like a million bucks for far less. Now out of the basement, Rags is a place where you can see Margaret's vision and standards in everything you touch. Her ambition for scale is evident in the systems that make Rags run like a tech company. Her commitment to the environment is in the model itself. She is a great businessperson, so she has a loyal and well-trained staff, but it is her energy and point of view that I feel most acutely when I am in the store.

Margaret has created my number-one retail experience. There is a woman neither I nor Margaret has ever met who delivers four to six giant bags of high-end designer clothing to Rags two times a year. When this happens, Margaret texts me to offer a personal showing. This consignor—whom I call my "fairy god-consignor"—is exactly my size. I get the first look at incredible couture items that are tailored perfectly for me and priced affordably because they are used. This is a win for all. I get to look hip; Rags gets an avid buyer for some of its high-end merchandise; and the fairy god-consignor works her side hustle. And all of this happens because Margaret is deeply involved in marketing and sales efforts.

AN EXAMPLE:
COFOUNDERS CREATING THE COMPANY CULTURE

Software engineers Quinn Slack and Beyang Liu founded Sourcegraph in 2013 to help make software development more efficient, effective, and enjoyable for coders. The founders successfully grew Sourcegraph over the next decade, selling the company's AI-driven software to individual developers and Fortune 100 companies. The company has all the departments one would expect in a software business—sales, marketing, customer success, and a raft of software engineers—but its culture continues to be driven by the founders themselves. Sourcegraph feels more like a developer-focused culture than any other tech company I've seen.

At this year's "Merge," a biannual in-person gathering for the company's distributed workforce, one morning began with a "cofounder code-off."

Slack and Liu had identified a new feature opportunity in the product, and they competed head-to-head in front of the entire company to see which of them could build the new feature faster. They were live coding for a crowd with their work captured on side-by-side big screens, similar to a Las Vegas sports book. Other companies might prioritize showing the staff the newest sales-pitch deck, the latest marketing messaging, or the design drawings for the new office, but Sourcegraph, because of its founders, puts coding at the center of the culture. The cofounders' personalities and talents are visible in everything this company does.

HUMILITY AS THE ENEMY OF SELLING ONESELF

One complicating factor in selling yourself is that many of us have had a lifetime of training in humility. Even the idea that you can intentionally sell yourself is anathema. I have spoken to people in different fields whom I see as archetypes of the art of selling themselves. They may be selling products, a new building fund for a nonprofit, or a vision to feed an under-resourced population. From most of them, when I asked if they also see themselves as the center of their sale, I received responses like "Oh, I know it's true that I'm at the center of the sale, but I don't want to say that publicly." Of course you won't sell effectively if you are uncontrollably arrogant, but you must be willing to share your talents and gifts openly to generate interest in a you-focused business.

Fletcher and Selling Software as His Authentic Self

Fletcher Richman started entrepreneurial selling early. At age twelve, he opened a lemonade stand in Aspen, Colorado. Instead of making the "best" lemonade, Fletcher bought the premade stuff, poured it into paper cups, and, knowing the likely wealth of Aspen passersby, sold each cup for $5. "I took the fastest path to see if the idea would work, and that rapid-iteration mentality is core to who I am," he says. He also knew what he was really selling: his passionate, enterprising twelve-year-old self.

Later, at the University of Colorado, he joined, incubated, and ultimately led many initiatives in the school's innovation ecosystem. He created three new business ideas over three years of CU's New Venture Challenge startup competition. He launched a nonprofit to build a coworking space for startups near campus, which he funded by pitching sponsorships to business leaders and companies. "I sold this opportunity unapologetically, putting myself at the center of it," he said. "Through a bunch of forwarded emails, our ask reached venture capitalist Brad Feld, and he emailed us within minutes saying he was in for $25,000." Fletcher's impact was so immense that CU created and awarded him the first Fletcher Richman Award for entrepreneurship.

A few years after graduating, Fletcher and two cofounders he had met at CU started a technology company ultimately called Halp. Halp was a support ticketing system for customer service and IT, all integrated into Slack, one of the most popular internal communications platforms in tech. "I have always been a productivity nerd who loves optimizing tools and integrating the best ones into a simple workflow," Fletcher says. As with his lemonade stand, Fletcher tested the idea of Halp with one LinkedIn post and a landing page. He thought both would be ignored. Within days, two hundred people had signed up to get on the wait list for a product that didn't exist. Six months later, the product launched, and Halp had its first paying customers.

Halp grew, and at every inflection point, Fletcher placed himself at the center of the action, leveraging his form of passionate ambivalence. Fletcher didn't apply, but Halp was later recruited to join the very competitive and prestigious Techstars Boulder Accelerator program.

The momentum continued, with Fletcher repeatedly re-creating an authentic pattern: being uninterested in doing things like raising money and then deciding to raise funds under great terms with ideal investors who offered. The company was growing well, adding blue-chip customers and never touching most of the cash it raised. Fletcher's sincere ambivalence made Halp extremely attractive to people who wanted to be a part of his success. His approach also built trust among Halp's investors and customers.

"Customers gravitated toward us because the IT people we were selling to were nerdy just like me in terms of productivity tools. I formed a personal bond with our buyers, and we enriched each other's lives by riffing on our favorite hacks," he says. "And my age worked for me. I was twenty-five, and Slack was still new for large companies, so we built a brand and a product that would make the life of IT people fun, using humor, emojis in support tickets, a goofy cat logo, and a connected community."

In March 2020, Fletcher received a cold email from the head of corporate development of software giant Atlassian. At the same time, he was in discussions about raising money the company didn't need with two of his dream investment funds. In a single week, Fletcher received term sheets from the investors for a new round of capital and from Atlassian for the acquisition of Halp. After testing Atlassian's commitment by pushing it to three times the initial offer price, Halp agreed to be bought in a very accretive transaction. Fletcher was actively retained by Atlassian in progressive product leadership roles for four years after the sale.

When I asked Fletcher how he forged this path, he said, "It is not in my nature to engage in gimmicks or schemes, staying four steps ahead of someone else and telling them what I think they want to hear to get to the outcome I want.

"I think my candor and my age worked for me. I could ask for help, and that often led to other great things, but the ask for help was real, not a manipulation."

ALL SELLING IS SUBJECTIVE

Many of us—especially people from underrepresented communities or disadvantaged populations in a given context—have been trained to downplay the parts of us that show up strongly when we sell from a starting point of our own strength. In addition, many of us have occasionally been rejected because of personal qualities that are unique (race, gender, upbringing). It's messy. I get it. I want to work with you to understand any negative self-talk, put it in its place at key times, and amplify the parts of you that are essential to growing your vision in a sales role or a comparable pursuit.

When I mention the idea of selling oneself, I'm often met with groans and grimaces. When I started down this path, I also believed the story that this type of sale was more challenging, more personal. I especially struggled with pricing, a topic I'll address at greater length later. The whole endeavor of self-selling felt subjective and arrogant. I eventually let most of that go, but it took some time. As other objective factors came into the frame—personal budget, a tight schedule born of success, knowledge of what my role models were charging—I grew more comfortable selling the subjective.

I now realize that *all selling is subjective!* Is your Software as a Service (SaaS) product for small businesses *objectively better than* your competitor's offering? Not always. When you're selling that SaaS product, or any product, the first thing to do is to develop an extremely accurate and detailed sense of what you are selling. What is the product? What is it great at? What problem does it solve? Where does it fail to deliver? Why is the product superior to others in the competitive set?

The second thing to do as a seller of a SaaS product is to dig into the kinds of customers that would benefit most from using it. For whom is this product perfect? What is the return on investment (ROI) for different kinds of prospective customers? What kinds of customers have tried this product and stayed with us? Which customers churned quickly after they purchased a subscription?

Next, a great salesperson listens for where the customers' needs intersect with the aspects of the product. All of these are subjective judgments derived from asking great questions, listening carefully, and problem solving with a potential customer. Finally, a salesperson must create a win-for-all deal, with pricing and features that are good for their company and the prospect they are pitching.

Selling yourself is identical.

Great selling of a business focused on you will feature the same key steps:

- Who are you? What are you great at? What value propositions of yours amount to the kinds of unique selling propositions (USPs) that a company might consider valuable?
- Who is your ideal customer profile (ICP)? What type of person, business, or other organization would benefit most from what you've outlined in the preceding bullet point?
- Once you manage to interest a potential ICP, you need to ask the questions and do the listening to determine whether you are a strong fit for each other.
- If there is mutual interest, create a project scope or a plan priced at a number that feels good for you and for them.

I'm oversimplifying, but I humbly suggest that if you treat yourself as the product and do *at least as much* inquiry about yourself, your USPs, your market, your ICP, and your packaging and pricing as you would for something other than you, you will make selling yourself feel more scientific and objective. The rest of this book will dig into every step of this process.

There is another nuance here. No matter *what it is that you are selling*, you are almost *always* selling *you* as part of the mix. So we are always in our own sales, whether we're selling a solopreneur business or something that seems more removed from who we are.

QUIETING YOUR IMPOSTER VOICE

Before we move along, I want to say something I hear every time I talk to people about selling themselves. They report they have an inner voice blurting "You can't," "You shouldn't," "You won't do a good job," "You're not worth that," or "If you charge less, they're more likely to say yes."

I know. I have an imposter voice, too. I call her Nancy. She's a persona. She's not bad. I don't want to get rid of her. When she's on her game (and I'm on mine), she can keep me from being arrogant and stubborn. She preserves in me a sense of self-doubt that can be extremely helpful when I'm righteously ranting. And she's *extremely unhelpful* when it comes to writing copy for my website, sending an email reply to a famous person who just reached out, or quoting a price for a gig in Australia that requires a ton of travel. Nancy can make me price my services too low in a way I might later resent. She tells me to book budget motels on business trips, because the client won't want to pay for something nicer and more convenient for me. She tries to convince me that I shouldn't reach out to that very impressive someone because that person probably gets a heap of incoming email requests and won't want to respond to me. When I let Nancy control *selling conversations*, I lose. So will you if you listen to your imposter voice.

I heard Elizabeth Gilbert, the internationally popular author, podcaster, and keynote speaker, speak a few years ago. She mentioned that her imposter voices had been having their way with her backstage. She then said something like "I listened to what my imposter voice had to say. I patted my imposter voice on the shoulder and told her I'd be back in forty-five minutes. I asked her to stay backstage and do her thing while I did mine. I said to her that 'these people didn't come here to listen to you, they came to listen to me.'" And then Liz came onstage.

That can work for you if you're selling yourself. Don't try to crush your imposter voice. It won't work, and it will deprive you of the value that a persona like this offers at other times. Get to know that imposter voice. Make friends with it. Give it a name. From this theoretical acquaintance, you will get the *choice* to defer to your imposter instincts or to choose a path that feels more courageous. That's the game I recommend when you're selling a business that is connected to you.

In the sales process, invite your imposter voice to take a lunch break as you step forward into the marketing, selling, and provision of the gifts that you uniquely have to offer.

EXERCISE
Selling Yourself, Simply

If selling yourself feels complicated, I recommend that you get very clear about your USP and your ICP. Much of this book will give you this clarity, but for now, try something on:

- Imagine that you are telling a nine-year-old about what you do and why you're good at it. Explain it to the kid in terms they will understand. Keep it short and interesting.
- Then imagine that the nine-year-old asks, "So who do you think will want to work with you?" And tell them in the same light and relatable way about your ideal client or customer.

PART 2

CLEARING THE BLOCKERS TO SUCCESS

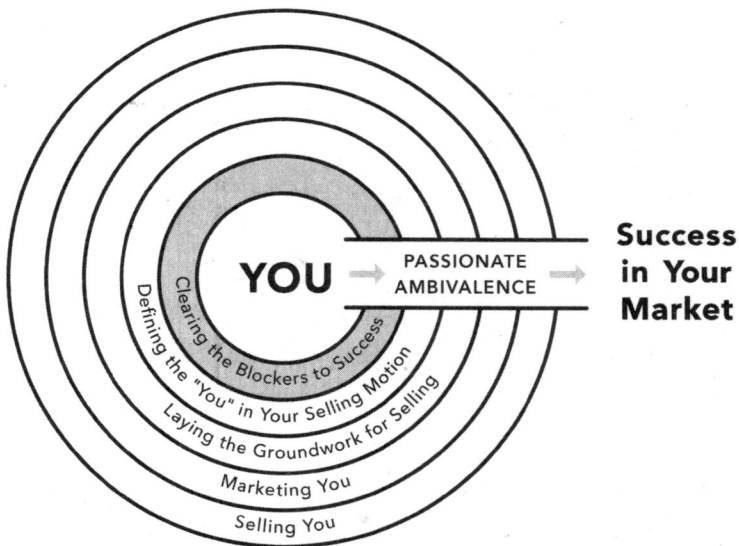

YOU → PASSIONATE AMBIVALENCE → Success in Your Market

Clearing the Blockers to Success
Defining the "You" in Your Selling Motion
Laying the Groundwork for Selling
Marketing You
Selling You

CHAPTER 4

UNDERSTANDING
UNCONSCIOUS COMMITMENTS

I love the concept of unconscious commitments. Unconscious commitments are a wonderful lens to reveal what you are actually committed to. One reason you may read this book, learn a ton, and continue generating subpar results is that you are unconsciously committed to staying right where you are.

I work as an executive coach with C-level leaders and teams, and I find attention to unconscious commitments to be the single most transformative tool in my kit. Only after your unconscious commitments are made conscious and visible can you address them.

To give you a sense of what unconscious commitments feel like, I want to share a personal example. As of this writing, I'm in my late fifties. I married briefly in my late twenties. When that ended, I spent over twenty-five years meeting people during the era of online dating. You've figured out that I love selling; you understand that I view almost everything as selling. One thing I view as a near-perfect example of selling is online dating. And I have been successful, meaning I've met terrific people and enjoyed meaningful relationships.

I approached the entire online dating endeavor as a market economy: heaps of inventory, with some friction in making the right matches between me and the "SKUs" on Match.com, Jdate, Tinder, Bumble, and Hinge. My goal always was to fall in love, but with chemistry being what it is, I figured it was a numbers game at the outset. So each time I was single and embarking on a mission to meet someone, I set up three-hour blocks at a coffee shop on a weekend day. I met six to ten men during each of those blocks, being completely transparent about my approach. I vetted. I sold with a heavy dose of passionate ambivalence (each date was one of many on that day, after all). And without fail, I eventually found love.

You would think I was fully committed to meeting a long-term partner. I thought I was, too. But every year or two, I would find myself unhappy in my partnership. I could be controlling. I could be hopelessly, aggressively independent. I could prioritize my work and friends over the interests of my boyfriends. As I saw a pattern of serial monogamy playing out over decades, I realized that I was *consciously committed* to meeting my long-term partner. Look at all the things I was doing to make that happen! But I was also prioritizing my own life and the freedom to do exactly what I wanted to do when I wanted to do it. I was *unconsciously committed* to being single.

I came to understand this and to see how I was getting in the way, not in how I was behaving but in the relationships I was forming. As of this writing, I'm happily and newly married to a man I "swiped right on" while sitting on the tarmac at a Chicago airport. He knows all about my unconscious patterns; we notice when they're activated and explore them. I know his unconscious patterns, too, and together we are getting closer by making the unconscious more conscious in service of having more choice about what we do next, together.

SHIFTING CORE PATTERNS TAKES AWARENESS AND EFFORT

Change is often unpleasant. This is true in the personal and the professional contexts. If you are running a business that is 50 percent as large as the business of your dreams, there are likely places where you are unconsciously committed to staying smaller than you say you want to be. It is comfortable, safe, and familiar to stay where you are. New ways threaten a stable system.

Great sellers pay attention to where their attachment to existing patterns will limit their greatest potential.

No one walks around talking about their unconscious commitments at parties. Really. Try this on: "I'm more attached to keeping my business small than I am to funding my kids' education" or "I'm giving up on the idea of winning a new piece of business with one of the companies I most admire because I'm scared the possible rejection may really hurt me."

Instead of looking at the choices we make in the shadows of our unconscious decision-making, we tout our conscious commitments. We make resolutions on January 1. We sign up for health-club memberships and announce that we will work out five days a week starting now. We talk about our commitments to changing our relationships with our spouse, a fading friend, or a parent. We get accountability partners to check our compliance. We buy journals to chart our progress. Sometimes we actually *do* the thing we are talking about doing. And sometimes we make a vague and tepid effort and then revert to old patterns. You can imagine how important this might be when it comes to growing your business and selling yourself. Let's face down some of this behavior by coming off autopilot.

If you want to know what you're *really* committed to, look at the results. What are you actually doing? How successful have you been in reaching the goals you set for your business? How intentional have you been in setting those goals? How many risky outreach messages have you sent on LinkedIn? If the answer to any of these questions is short of what you'd like it to be, you likely are unconsciously committed to doing exactly what you're doing: not quite meeting the objectives you talk about meeting.

OWNING UNCONSCIOUS COMMITMENTS IN SALES

An example of an unconscious commitment that appears in selling contexts is a commitment to avoiding meaningful rejection. I alluded to this earlier, but this one is so prevalent that it's worth further consideration. There are many ways of selling that do not involve a perceived threat to one's ego: marketing a product or service on LinkedIn versus through direct asks; setting up automatic email campaigns and buying email lists of people who are in your target customer set but are strangers to you; or glibly eliding a true answer at a gathering of friends about what you're doing for work and your interest in bringing on more clients. These behaviors could result in sales, and you can tell yourself and your friends that you are out there "selling." But none of these more passive strategies is vulnerable. If no one responds to your push email campaigns, you won't take it personally. If your dinner-party companions don't follow up to ask you about working together, you can write it off because you know how blasé you were in talking about your work. So your conscious commitment is to drive sales, but your unconscious commitment is to put a fishing line in the water and go have lunch, to sell in ways that are designed to protect your self-image and keep you in a comfort zone of personal risk. This unconscious commitment—to passive selling versus active, risky engagement where you put yourself out there in a way that might cause you to feel ignored or hurt—is a major limiting factor on your ability to grow your business.

Instead of blaming or shaming yourself for these quite understandable, previously unconscious coping strategies, the first order of business as a conscious seller of yourself is to own your unconscious commitments. In doing so, you can uncover the underlying motivations that keep you on a path that isn't meeting your stated, conscious expectations.

The first step to understanding your unconscious commitments is to look for places where you say you want X and instead have Y. Say you want to hit $200,000 in annual revenue this year. It might be November, and you might be tracking toward $120,000. In normal human parlance, you might say, "I am committed to hitting $200,000, but I'm missing that goal, and I'm likely going to hit $120,000 instead." That's no problem. It's fine.

But let's try it a different way. Remember that you are a high-functioning human (you are superb, remember?). As such, if you're hitting $120,000, the notion of unconscious commitments suggests that at some level, you are *choosing* $120,000 or *committed to* generating $120,000 in revenue this year.

I realize this sounds ridiculous. It's much easier to believe the missed revenue target is happening "to you" based on the economy, a contract that never got signed, and forty other things. My suggestion, however, is that as a conscious seller, you let go of the excuses and simply own that whatever is happening is exactly what you are committed to. The best way to understand what we're truly committed to is to look at the results.

SPOTTING THE UNCONSCIOUS BENEFITS FROM YOUR PATTERNS

Once you've noticed where you might have an unconscious commitment, the next step is to understand what benefit you have been getting (unconsciously) by manifesting your current results. It's a tricky exercise because the benefit is in the shadows, but if you're living out unconscious commitments, there is surely a way that the seemingly undesired circumstance is actually serving you.

Let's take a common unconscious commitment that I often see in sellers. Some people are unconsciously committed to playing small. They underprice their work, they start a new company that isn't as daring as it might be, or they stay silent instead of sharing their authentic points of view. Because the idea of playing small can seem amorphous, I'd like to share two examples of this behavior:

1. I worked closely with a senior leader in HR who had been with her company for four years. In her third year, the company hired an older, more globally well-known leader to take the helm of the HR organization. The big selling point for this leader was that his international brand would make him an effective ambassador to the HR industry, which was the target customer for the company. My client was handling what seemed like 95 percent of all HR leadership functions. She was the person to whom all other leaders went if they had an HR issue or opportunity, but she held the number-two job. Doing all the work without the concomitant recognition strikes me as playing small.

2. When the MergeLane Fund was actively making investments from 2014 to 2024, we routinely received pitches for investment. Even during times of relative abundance in the VC funding

space—where early companies were raising first rounds of capital of $1 million or more—there was a subset of founders who
were trying to raise $75,000. My sense (and our fund's sense)
was that asking venture capitalists for a relatively paltry sum
suggested that those founders were not ambitious enough about
scaling their early businesses. They seemed to be playing small.

I sum up these behaviors as playing small, which is a unique and special trigger for me. "You spot it, you got it" is a reliable truism, so I'm sure
it bothers me because I also do it. When I play small, it is usually an outgrowth of letting my imposter voice or my inner critic run the show, thinking I'm not quite good enough to win that client and then underpricing the
work because if I get it, it will be a real feather in my cap. I almost *always*
resent small-game decisions later, and, as I'll share later in this book, playing
small often leaves me *less* rather than *more* likely to get the work.

But if you play small, as I do at times, ask yourself, what are the benefits
of that approach? I can feel you rolling your eyes as you read this, but stay
with me. Benefits of playing small might include

- Comfort with staying in familiar territory
- Avoiding risk
- Avoiding conflict
- Deferring accountability
- Being part of the gang that is accustomed to seeing you in a cer-
  tain way
- Enjoying the help other people want to give you
- Being liked
- Avoiding rejection or failure
- Continuing to work with your current clients, colleagues, or
  mentors
- Indulging your inner critic

Armed with the benefits of your unconscious commitment, it should
be easy to accept yourself for this under-the-covers pattern you've been

perpetrating. Once you reach that understanding with yourself, you can wonder what the unconscious commitment is costing you. Playing small in your sales effort or your business often costs you personal growth, financial freedom, and major opportunities to learn.

FROM AWARENESS TO ACTIONABLE UNDERSTANDING

There may be more. Playing small may just be the start. You may also be committed to undermining your growth, freedom, and learning. No problem. The game is to grow your awareness and understanding about your patterns to give you a fighting chance of shifting them from autopilot to awareness and agency. When you understand your unconscious commitments, you gain more choice about how to act and react in various situations.

This awareness is a big deal. If you're playing along here, you are likely looking at one or more deep, abiding patterns that cut across your lifetime and many areas of your life, both personal and professional. To prompt your understanding of this conceptual framework for yourself, consider a few questions:

+ In what kinds of situations am I most triggered—fearful or angry?
+ When I get into that triggered state, what is my most common reaction? Where do I go for "safety," or what is my habitual response to that trigger?
+ What is something I say I really want that I consistently do not have or do? How am I perpetuating a situation where I do not have or do the thing I say I want?

Noticing these unconscious behaviors is huge. Being willing to consider changing them—when they may have helped you manifest many things in your life that you really wanted—is beyond courageous. It's a ninja move.

Once you understand an unconscious commitment or two, and the associated costs and benefits, it's time to reach for the next level of mastery.

SEEING A CORE COMMITMENT IN EVERY AREA OF LIFE

You can become even smarter about unconscious commitments by noticing how beautifully you've been supporting those commitments across your life. Imagine that you were trying to teach a class of newbies how to create your unconscious commitment across a lifetime in exactly the way you have done it. The lesson plan here can involve big and small efforts you make in support of an unconscious commitment.

The purpose of this exercise is not self-flagellation; it is, again, awareness. When you acknowledge unconscious commitments and dig deeper to become clear on all the ways you solidify and reinforce your unconscious commitments, you gain the ability to spot the less productive aspects of your pattern in the smallest details. You can see your unconscious commitment in practice and gain a greater ability to interrupt it by noticing the minutiae that underlie it.

One of my clients had a unique version of playing small as a core unconscious commitment. He was the head of product development at a fast-growing tech company, and he discovered that he had an unconscious commitment to being deferential. He took my invitation to notice the prominence of that commitment across his life. He did his homework, and then I asked him to teach me how to be a deferential leader and person in just the way he had been doing it. Again, the goals of this exercise were to increase his awareness, to see how his shady motivations were showing up in this core pattern, and to give him more choice in the future over how he showed up as a leader, partner, and parent.

My client did that deep dive, and I'll share it with you. If you have an unconscious tendency toward deference, some of these may sound familiar. If you have another unconscious tendency, this list will show you how to flesh out your commitment. Remember, he's teaching me (and now you) how he does it, so this is phrased in the second person:

- If anyone calls out a deficiency or something you did wrong, immediately deflect with a joke.
- If someone comes to you with a tough question, immediately tell them to ask the person who they think should make the call (and not you).

- When asked about something you have not planned, do not lead with your instinct, but deflect and get others' opinions first.
- Anytime a request comes in from the sales team, do not evaluate the importance of the request. Just drop everything and work on it.
- When entering a new space filled with people you don't know, hold back to observe.
- If you have a plan that may rock the boat, shop it around first to get others on board.
- If someone pushes back strongly, don't challenge them. Assume they have prepared more than you, and go with their recommendation.
- If arguments occur, don't let them continue. Look for common ground to create consensus and closure as quickly as possible to avoid confrontation.
- If you get an email, Slack message, or call from your boss or any peer—no matter what it is about—answer it as quickly as possible so you can help.
- When business needs trump your personal career needs, always put your personal plans aside to serve the business.
- When you have the choice to adapt to the situation or push for change, always adapt.
- Hold your opinions loosely—everyone else's are more important.
- If you miss a deadline, immediately think of all the ways you could have given up more of your personal time to achieve it, shame yourself, and push harder next time.
- If someone else misses a deadline, immediately think of all the ways their personal life could have caused them to fail to achieve it, and empathize with them.

If you have identified an unconscious commitment, you can do a similar exercise to evaluate all the ways in which it has been permeating your life and burrowing its way into your patterns of behavior, personality, and relationships.

FROM AUTOPILOT TO CHOICE

Once you have learned all the ways in which you've been interfering with reaching your conscious commitment (often your full potential), you have choices. And choices are gold. The first—and most important—choice is whether you are willing to shift. This need not be a full U-turn, but some tweaks will be necessary. Ask whether you're willing to take the risk of being honest with yourself and others about your pattern. Are you game to commit to pausing in familiar situations where your unconscious commitment might previously have led you to behave in a patterned way? Will you endeavor to let go of the comfort of doing it the way you have been for quite some time and instead consider other options that are surely more difficult, if only because they're less familiar? Shedding unconscious commitments is uncomfortable and scary because often you don't know what might happen if you cast off your historically unconscious script.

For the record, you may also decide that you are not willing to shift. You may instead be honest with yourself about whether your stated or conscious goal was even a good fit for you or whether you were on autopilot when you set that goal. Perhaps your goal of waking up at 5 a.m. was inspired by all those articles on how to hack your productivity, but you do your best work in the late afternoon. Or you thought you wanted to be promoted to the head of your department for the status and salary bump, but you skipped over the fact that managing others is way less exciting to you than doing the real work. But if you are certain that your goals are the right targets for you and you've found the ways you've been sabotaging yourself, then eventually you will return to the option of shifting an old pattern.

If you decide you *are* willing to shift a pattern, then you will get to make that choice again each time you pause, realizing you're about to engage in your once unconscious pattern. In that space of awareness, you can choose something else. That something else is usually being honest, letting go of control, or shedding concern about whether others like or approve of you. It's not for the faint of heart, but it's well worth it to gain more agency, choice, and access to your highest potential.

Every element of this concept of unconscious commitments is intended to help you see how you get in the way of reaching your goals. The better you know your core patterns and how they serve you—or don't—the faster you can shift to more productive patterns that will help you meet your true objectives.

EXERCISE

Understanding Your Unconscious Commitments

+ Think of one of your unconscious commitments that is associated with growing your business, sales success, or career. Ask yourself, "What result do I regularly complain about that never seems to change?" You'll know you've uncovered an unconscious commitment when you find a consistent behavior or result in your life that you wouldn't want to talk about on a first date or at a family holiday dinner.

+ Own your commitment. Out loud. Start with "I am committed to …" For example, "I am committed to marketing my services to companies that cannot pay me what I am worth."

+ Imagine that you want to teach someone how to create or manifest your unconscious commitment just like you. Make a few notes for how you would teach them to do it your way. For example, "I email my friends in nonprofit organizations about what I do because that is less intimidating than contacting my friends in large companies."

+ Once you have that in mind, identify the benefits you're getting from your (previously) unconscious commitment. How does that commitment serve you? For example, "I don't have to face the fear of rejection from my friends who have really 'made it in the world.'"

+ Name one or two ways in which your unconscious commitment has cost or disserved you. For example, "All of my friends in nonprofits are struggling due to the downturn in charitable giving, and they are lowering rates paid to consultants."

+ What would you need to risk to upend this previously unconscious commitment? For example, "I would need to be willing to risk embarrassment."

+ Are you willing to take the risk or risks you just named? The answer may be no. That's fine. The next time you consider complaining about this situation, you can remind yourself of the ways that you are engineering it. If the answer is yes, then jot down a positive conscious commitment representing a large or small shift that you are willing to make: "I am committed to seeing myself as an equal to my friends in corporate jobs and to emailing two of them in the next two weeks about my business."[2]

---

2   Some of this language is derived from exercises crafted by Kaley Klemp and Devon Tivona.

CHAPTER 5

ADDRESSING LIMITING BELIEFS

A specific form of unconscious commitment is commonly called a limiting belief. We develop limiting beliefs in all sorts of ways. You may have heard some negative messaging about yourself from a parent or an influential teacher early on. Your culture may have some implicit thesis about what people who resemble you should do in life and business. On my most recent binge watch of my favorite dating reality show, a man said to a woman, "I am sure people hear your voice and think you're not very smart, but I see how smart you are." His dismissive comment contains layers of limiting beliefs (projected onto someone else), and those kinds of statements can stick.

A former senior executive client of mine told me she liked to feel that she was performing at a level about 25 percent higher than her salary. That buffer made her feel insulated from accusations of underperforming. Her limiting belief was that if she were paid in accordance with her actual contribution, she would be exposed to insult or, worse, demotion or termination.

To identify and clear the barriers to becoming a confident seller who can ably deploy the technique of passionate ambivalence, you will want to identify and interrogate any limiting beliefs that undermine your success.

Your limiting beliefs may sound like the following:

- People who do _____ for a living are poor.
- No one is spending money during this economic downturn, so I won't be able to sell my services.

+ I don't have the required training to _____.
+ I'm not old enough to _____.
+ I'm too old to _____.
+ It's harder for female CEOs to raise VC funding.
+ Doing this thing has to be difficult; anything easy must be an impermissible shortcut.
+ I haven't been able to do _____ in the past, so I won't be able to do it in the future.
+ People who do _____ need to have impressive educational backgrounds.
+ I don't have enough executive presence to influence people more senior than I am.
+ Given this personality trait of mine, I'm never going to be a good _____.
+ The only path to real success is to be an executive.
+ There are already way too many coaches.

Growing a business while harboring limiting beliefs like these is difficult at best and impossible at worst. These beliefs create a tremendous drag in the system. You want your system focused on success. To get that focus, you want to become familiar with these limiting beliefs, assess objectively whether they are actually "true," gain more understanding of how much control they may have over you, and find a way to hold them more loosely.

EXERCISE
Identify and Test Your Limiting Beliefs

Here's an exercise to get started. Under each prompt, I've offered an example of the answers from organizational development PhD and solopreneur Julia Wiener. Her reflections should help you generate your own ideas.

Step One: Write a list of three to five limiting beliefs that may be affecting you and your ability to achieve your goals. Be honest. Some of these may not seem directly relevant to selling, but jot them down anyway. They may have a greater impact than you think. If this step feels hard to understand, consider this lens: As you think about achieving your goals, what "buts" come up for you? Finish the sentence "I would totally achieve my goal of X, *but*..."

Julia: I would totally achieve my goal of consulting with private equity (PE) firms, but...

+ I don't have proven experience.
+ I'm not associated with a global consulting firm.
+ Potential customers probably already have their favorite consultants.
+ I don't look like the traditional person who is interested in PE and mergers and acquisitions.
+ I'm a relative unknown. I don't have many strong contacts in this industry, a big social media following, or a best-selling book.

Step Two: Try to identify the source of each limiting belief. Start with the one that feels most true to you. Where did you hear or learn it? Then consider whether the source of this belief was credible. Was there quality data supporting the assertion, or is it something one person said on social media with a ton of conviction? Why did this belief stick with you?

Julia: I don't have proven experience.

This belief sticks with me because I believe that I must earn opportunities through hard work and proving that I am capable. When applying for a promotion in the early days of my career, I remember trusted mentors telling me that a company wants to see that you can do your current job and more before granting a promotion. I have treated this as biblical ever since, endeavoring to prove myself beyond what was expected to show I was "good enough." My mom told me as a kid that I had to work twice as hard as my peers:

once because I am female and twice because I am black. Therefore, just having a small amount of experience isn't enough; I feel like I need years of success in a specific industry to work in it.

Step Three: For each limiting belief, ask yourself whether the belief is true in any objective sense. Then ask yourself whether the opposite of your limiting belief may be as true as or truer than your belief. For example, the opposite of "I am too young to _____" might be "I am the right age to _____." That's not the exact opposite, but let's not quibble.

Julia: I don't have proven experience.

Yes, this belief seems objectively true. Although a company I co-owned was evaluated by PE firms during talks that resulted in an acquisition of our firm, I have not had experience providing consulting services to a PE firm.

However, when I look at "I do have proven experience," I can see that it is also quite true. During the acquisition process, I had meaningful exposure to prospective PE buyers, and they ascribed the quality of our company culture to me.

Step Four: When you look at the opposing statements, see if you can find a few examples in the world that support the truth of each one. For example, if one of your limiting beliefs is that you are too young to start a new company, the opposite might be "I am the right age to start a new company." Two possible examples supporting the truth of that opposite statement are as follows: Mark Zuckerberg started Facebook (now Meta) when he was nineteen years old; I have more flexibility at this age because I am on my own without responsibility for a partner, older parents, or young children.

Engaging in the practice of finding evidence to support the views that are the opposite of your central limiting beliefs will help you create more space around these limiting beliefs. You will also gain a better understanding of how often these beliefs reside in you as absolutes and potentially control your actions and outlook.[3]

Julia: I have a wealth of experience providing the type of consulting I want to provide to PE firms.

+ Everyone who works in consulting for PE firms had a first day. Before that first day, they, too, had no experience working for PE firms.
+ Perhaps not having specific experience with PE firms is a good thing. I bring a fresh perspective. I also have foundations of theoretical knowledge and real-life experience.

Step Five: Armed with an improved understanding of your limiting beliefs and an evaluation of the merit of at least one of them, give yourself a choice. If your limiting beliefs, upon further examination, are true(ish), you may choose to opt out of your current pursuit or pivot to something that seems to be a sounder choice for you based on the data. If, on the other hand, your beliefs are not as true as you might have guessed, weed them out early and often so you're not in a constant struggle to prevail against them. Achieving your goals is plenty of work without carting around a bunch of specious, insidious baggage.

---

3   This approach is drawn in part from The Work by Byron Katie, www.thework.org.

CHAPTER 6

UPPER LIMITS

One of the most common ways I see unconscious commitments play out is when people are restricted by their unconscious upper limits. As you're reading this book, you may have thoughts like "This isn't for me," "This will never work in my business," "I can't be that confident," or "I can't charge that much." Those, my friends, are just a few of the hundreds of upper-limit thoughts one might have in exploring opportunities to grow oneself or one's business. Heck, I had thousands of upper-limit thoughts in writing this book! But upper limits can be transformative. In his book *The Big Leap: Conquer Your Hidden Fear and Take Life to the Next Level*, Gay Hendricks addresses this directly.

The concept is that each of us carries ingrained, unconscious ideas of just how happy and successful we can be. There's a sense over our lifetimes of a ceiling on joy, connectedness, love, and success. These ideas start early, such as when a parent tells a child to calm down at the playground because they might get hurt. You may have received early messages about how much you can progress in a career given one theoretical limitation or another. As we become more entrenched in our lives, we incorporate these background notions into our way of being, imagining in moments of peak joy or accomplishment that "the other shoe is about to fall," "we'll see how long that lasts," or "I'm crazy about him, but we're just in the honeymoon phase."

Gay Hendricks identifies four types of upper-limit problems, or hidden barriers. I've listed the following four, along with a little context to illustrate how that upper-limit problem might show up in your sales efforts.

1. **Feeling Fundamentally Flawed:** I have a big chance at a new client, but I will never be successful in landing them. They see me as a superstar, but they're wrong. They just haven't figured out yet that I only look good at first until my true colors shine. Eventually, likely before we ink this deal, they will see that they've made an error, and I will be out.

2. **Disloyalty or Abandonment:** If I shine more brightly in my business, my family or my high school friends will think I'm being disloyal to them. I should stay in my lane, be seen as one of the gang, and tamp down my hopes and expectations so I can preserve those relationships.

3. **Belief That More Success Makes You a Bigger Burden:** Whenever I have a big breakthrough at work and things are going really well, it usually requires that I put in more hours and be more focused, which means my partner pitches in more and I don't see my friends as much. I'm sure they resent me for that. If I dial down my successes, then I won't feel so much guilt for being a burden.

4. **The Crime of Outshining:** I'm thinking of starting this new company, and prospective customers are really juiced about it. I have three customers ready to sign as soon as I green-light my venture and leave my day job. But if I make this big change, I'm going to make people I care about (like my current team members) feel inferior, and I don't think I should cause them that kind of pain. So I'll steer clear of this big opportunity to save my intimates from feeling small in relation to me.

Upper-limit thoughts that extend to the ways you conduct yourself in selling your you-focused business create a much tougher road ahead. You may get close to an unexpected success and consciously or unconsciously undermine your likelihood of achieving it.

DEVELOP AWARENESS

It is not easy to become aware of something that has heretofore been unconscious, but you are probably getting warmed up to this game by now. You
can recognize that an upper-limit thought might be at play when you come
close to having or achieving something you want. Then something happens
(you do a thing, or a thing just occurs) that keeps you from reaching that
objective at the last instant. This near miss might occur for any of the four
upper-limit reasons shared earlier.

For example, I was recently coaching a client about a promotion conversation she wanted to have with her boss. She had a list of ten reasons that
she deserved the promotion. Just after she ticked off those reasons in preparation for her big chat with her boss, she said, "But really, I don't deserve
this promotion and probably won't get it because I don't meet the experience requirement for the more senior role." This conversation followed the
curve of an upper-limit thought sequence. My client was energized when
she shared her justifications for promotion, and then she metaphorically
knocked herself down with her upper-limit thought of not being enough.

Years ago, I was eager to have the honor of introducing a company I had
mentored at an annual Techstars startup program culmination event, Demo
Day. It was a big deal to be asked to be the presenting mentor for a company. One
year, one of my mentee companies asked me. Within fifteen seconds, I experienced the high of being asked followed by the immediate low of an upper-limit
thought. What I said instead of yes was "Thank you, but you should choose
someone with more status in this community to send a strong signal to investors." They chose someone else at my suggestion. My upper limit and I took me
right out of the running. I only had to torture myself for a year before another
company asked me to take the stage. That time I gave a full-throated yes.

NOTICE THAT OTHER-SHOE-DROPPED AFTEREFFECT

Another common example that may help you recognize an upper limit is the
experience of doing something fantastic, having a great time, and following
that experiential high with a big fight with a partner, parent, or coworker.

What you want is to take that high home with you. What you get is an interruption of your joy by unconsciously creating something that takes you down an emotional peg. It is these kinds of peaks and valleys that best signal the presence of upper limits.

EXERCISE
Identify Upper Limits in Selling

Try these steps to recognize and address upper limits with a specific focus on sales, your business, or any other goal you are chasing.

Step One: Think of a goal you are pursuing, and honestly assess how well you've done in reaching it or progressing toward it.

Step Two: As you think about the goal and your presumed inability to reach it (yet), tune into your feelings and the sensations in your body. If you notice that you have developed an unconscious ceiling for success and happiness, you might start to sense a physical tightness or contraction that arises as you think about this goal. You may see that you are literally or figuratively setting yourself up for stubbing your toe leading up to or immediately after a key milestone or a big win.

Step Three: As you become more familiar with your upper limits (thoughts, behaviors, feelings), presumably linked to the achievement of this objective, start to break down the connection between the win and the proverbial stubbed toe. Analyze your situation as if you were an outsider, and endeavor to spot any false connection you have made between your current activities or mindset and your advancement toward your goal.

Step Four: Try to identify which core patterns or unconscious commitments are holding your upper limits in place. Upper limits often keep us from leaning into our zone of genius, a topic I'll discuss more in the next section. You can begin to chip away at upper limits as you start to understand your specific personality patterns in this arena.

Step Five: Going forward, when you notice upper-limit thoughts as you sell—when you find yourself thinking you couldn't possibly enjoy the level of success and satisfaction this book lays out for you—do something grounding. Sweep the floor, go for a walk, take a few deep breaths, or write in a journal. Endeavor to interrupt the connection between goal attainment and impediments. Other grounding exercises are more specific to the context of selling: Write a blog post, send a few outreach emails, send connection requests on LinkedIn, or ask a recent client for a testimonial.

As I embarked upon writing this book, I experienced the upper-limit problem of feeling fundamentally flawed. I had the thought that whatever "shitty first draft"[4] I was writing was even shittier than I thought it was. The draft was complete bunk. My 60,000-word manuscript would have exactly 335 words of value. I had a few good moments of sharing the content of this book in 1:1 settings and one workshop, but those are distant memories, and they were edge cases.

My second upper limit in writing this book was the exact opposite of this fear of failure. It was the fear of success that underlies many upper limits. If I were to write something meaningful, if I were drawn to writing, I might do something great. If I were to do that, then how could I explain the ten to twenty years in which I've been unable to put font to digital paper? How many books have I missed? How bad have my career and personal choices been to have kept me from this pursuit? This upper-limit thought prompted some mental patter: "I really want to write. Look over at that office and how appealing that setup looks for writing right now. Notice how yummy it feels that this book is being written through me, like a river. *Yuck.* I can't allow this. No. Something must be *wrong!*"

When you make your unconscious ceiling conscious, you have a shot at raising your ceiling. If you don't do that, you will keep yourself from becoming a stellar seller of you and your you-focused business. No one wants that!

---

4   Anne Lamott, *Bird by Bird: Some Instructions on Writing and Life* (Anchor, 2007).

Wawira Njiru, Founder, Food for Education

Wawira Njiru started Food for Education (FFE), a nonprofit that feeds schoolchildren across Kenya, during her final year of university. Wawira is selling a mission of bolstering healthy, educated kids using her smarts, charm, and tireless dedication as tools for selling her gigantic vision.

Initially, she thought of it as a small passion project. She raised money through friends and family, selling the concept that by donating just $10 or $20, an individual could make a difference in a young person's life. FFE started by providing twenty-five children with a daily lunch.

When Wawira finished college, she plunged into FFE full-time. She went from feeding twenty-five kids to feeding one hundred. Then one thousand felt doable. FFE is Kenya's largest food operation. As of 2024, it is feeding 300,000 children each day with a goal of feeding three million across three African countries by 2030.

Wawira has routinely needed to raise money to support this growth. Fundraising is her version of selling, and she hates the "selling yourself" part. Yet she's become phenomenally good at it. "At the beginning," she says, "I had to really figure out what my story was, what my connection was to the work.

"I didn't grow up hungry. I was raised middle class," Wawira says. "And the reason I do this is because I'm Kenyan, and this is my country, and I was frustrated. I felt someone's got to do something. And there was no one around me who was raising their hand to do it.

"Telling my story was about pulling parts of me together that made it logical for me to do this. I run a large-scale food operation, so being a nutritionist gave me credibility in talking about protein formulation," she says. "As successful as we have been raising interest and funding for this project, I'm still navigating that comfort around selling myself."

In 2016, FFE received its first institutional grant from a foundation thanks to a cold call and a proposal Wawira wrote. "That win was an outgrowth of a lot of practice in failing and slowly learning how to make something feel familiar and compelling to a funder. That first grant was about $60,000. I was blown away that somebody would give us $60,000."

The next big breakthrough was joining a Silicon Valley accelerator program. "I went to Silicon Valley, and I was humble," she says. "Kenyans are very humble. And then you go to America, where everyone is selling themselves and talking about how they're saving the world. And I thought, *How can you say you're saving the world? It's so big!*

"I remember the final pitch event at the accelerator," she says. Wawira planned to ask for $100,000. "If we got that, we'd be really happy because the most we had ever raised was $60,000." Until one of the program mentors told her, "You can't go to an investor showcase in Silicon Valley and ask for $100,000. You have to have a bigger number." That mentor helped her craft an ask for $350,000. She got it.

"That was a big shift for me in terms of selling myself," she says. She learned to sell using the language of growth, of investors and funders. "I talked not just about hungry kids but also about ROI."

Now, before making a pitch to a funder, she asks herself, "Am I talking to someone who has $100,000, or am I talking to someone who has $300,000? If someone has $300,000, I adjust my pitch to that goal versus selling myself short for just $100,000. And that was an important lesson."

Today, FFE has four thousand team members. "One thing I'm sort of scared of or concerned about is what happens when we are feeding one million students a day? Once you hit your goal," she says, "do you make a new goal? Do I keep going? Do I let someone else take over?"

"Obviously, our growth is great for the kids. My question is around myself and what kind of leader I want to be."

EXERCISE
Exploring Your Upper Limits

- Complete the exercise on pages 47–48.
- Write a paragraph about a time in your life when you experienced an upper-limit thought. To which of the four upper-limit problems would you ascribe that experience?
- If that situation arose again today, how might you think about those unhelpful thoughts given your newfound understanding of upper limits?

PART 3

DEFINING THE "YOU" IN YOUR SELLING MOTION

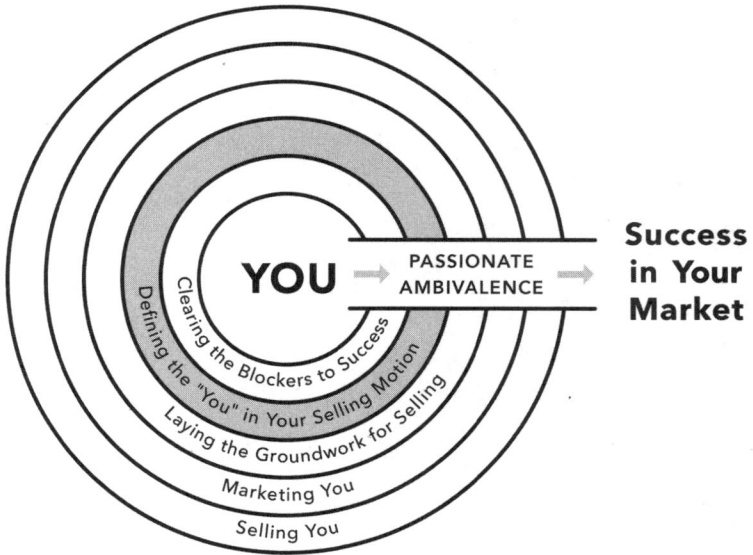

CHAPTER 7

YOUR PERSONAL BOARD OF DIRECTORS

When I was ready to leave my last executive role and start my own company, I received an extraordinary gift. At the time, I was a part of the first Conscious Leadership Forum, led by Jim Dethmer and Diana Chapman, the cofounders of the Conscious Leadership Group (CLG). This forum met quarterly. We were intimately connected, fully in support of the personal growth of ourselves, each other, and the forum.

During the forum session in which I shared my plan to strike out on my own, Diana made a life-altering suggestion: "What if we conduct our next forum in Boulder [my hometown], and we spend a full day of our planned retreat working as your personal board of directors?" Huh? Are you kidding me? These were fiercely talented, values-aligned humans. They had their own proverbial fish to fry, demanding jobs, and personal issues on which they were focused. The idea felt like "too much," but I knew not to let my imposter voice interfere with the best offer I was going to get for decades. As with most of Diana's suggestions to a group, everyone loved the idea and committed to joining the meeting.

Two months later, we gathered at a coworking space. Ten people who knew me very well put their attention on me, my highest potential, my gifts in the world, and my wish to create a joyful, enriching, full, and free life through this new endeavor. I prepared for that session. I created an agenda that incorporated a review of my goals (for our time together and for the first three years of my business), my planned service offerings, my brand, my values, my target customer, and my pricing strategy. Because these people were there to serve me, I included some fun activities and very good food and drink.

In what comes next, I will ask you to dig deeply into who you are. The work outlined in the next few chapters is primarily an inside job. But if you have the luxury of being surrounded by one or more talented, generous people who really get you and understand your business, recruit them for your personal and informal board of directors. Ask them for a day. Ask them for their honest reflections on you, your gifts, and your blind spots. Ask them to think about the things that light you up and help you thrive. Ask them how they think your gifts intersect with market needs and value creation in the world. Then listen.

My most valuable lesson from my meeting was to be honest, as a coach and facilitator, about whom I was for and whom I was not for. In fleshing out my core wants and values with this group, I said something like "I can't stand working around people who move slowly. It's boring. I want to work with people who, like me, relish change and can make changes quickly, even if not every change has a perfect outcome." The phrase that rang in this meeting: I only wanted to work with racehorses. When this popped out in the room, I felt nervous and shy. Can I say this? It's aggressive. It's not inclusive. It's not even necessarily always fantastic to *be* a racehorse. There are equally valid ways of being.

My board of directors did not shirk their responsibility in the face of my hesitation. They had seen my strains in my previous jobs. They knew that I was (at last) willing to be happy in my work, engaged in a pursuit that lit me up. To build a successful business focused primarily on me, I wanted to be absolutely clear about my preferences and willing to make tough decisions about work based on those preferences. I also *wanted to attract the racehorses*. Racehorses, metaphorically, were then and are now kindred to me.

Because *I am a racehorse*, I acted quickly and meaningfully on this insight. An early website page shouted, "I ONLY WORK WITH RACEHORSES," alongside a photo of some sweaty horses coming off the starting line. Later versions eliminated the dubious animal rights references, but every version of my business website since that first day has led with messages of speed and fearless willingness to change. Hero image phrases have included "Ready to Play a Bigger

Game?" (beach volleyball photo), "Activating Your Greatest Potential" (fire-works), and "Reimagining What's Possible" (fit woman looking over a canyon wall). Every one of these messages felt like me, and most of them came from reflections of that board of directors meeting more than ten years ago.

David Secunda and His "Tiger Team"

David Secunda is the founder of multiple startups who has used informal boards of advisors many times in his career. This year, David had a concrete, time-sensitive decision to make about the future of Avid for Adventure, a company he had founded in 2004 that was now at a critical inflection point. The company ran camps in four western states, including David's home state of Colorado.

Ten years after founding Avid and achieving strong economic performance and geographic and program expansion, David stepped away from the CEO role to start a new technology company, Workbright. "My strength is the first seven years of a company," David says. "I love the early ideation and co-creation. Once things get operationalized, I tend to get bored. I had a new idea, and I also felt that my departure would create room for others to grow in their roles." David founded Work-bright to solve the administrative challenges faced by companies, including Avid, that needed to rapidly hire seasonal employees.

A decade into growing Workbright, David began to think that Avid, which he still owned, was at a crossroads. The company had experienced its first downturn in its history. "One of my close business associates suggested I form a 'tiger team,'" says David. "I had no idea what that was, but I learned it was an informal group of advisors I could gather to help me think through the next steps in Avid's journey."

He invited ten people to advise him over the next week. He did not choose them based on domain expertise (though he got plenty of that). Instead, he selected people whom he valued for their wisdom and their willingness to share their honest views of the situation. "I wanted people who would tell it like it is," he says. "And that is definitely what I got." David also took advice from his adult daughter, who encour-aged him to "start at the top," choosing the people he felt would be most helpful, even if he wasn't sure how those people would react. All ten said yes.

David prepared a transparent six-page memo outlining the history and cur-rent state of the business. In the memo, he asked his readers to focus on three tactical questions: Which of two in-seat managers should be appointed to lead the company? Should the company continue operating in four states or dial back to just Colorado? Should the company consider a sale of the business? He scheduled three meetings with subsets of the larger group to get reflections from his advisors.

"What I set up as a decision-making process about staffing and geography became much more," he said. "The conversations became expansive, connected, personal, and deep. What does the company mean to me? How much do I care about my vision for what Avid can be in the future?"

At the start of one meeting, someone asked David if he was willing to eliminate camps outside Colorado. "I had an immediate no," he says. "Then that same advisor said, 'David, get over it. If you want the company to be what you say you want, then you are the only person to do that. Now, let's talk about that path.' So, five minutes into one meeting, I realized I was going to reject my proposed options and choose something I originally was against, taking over myself and getting the company back on track for future growth. I would not have reached that decision if I didn't have a circle of engaged truth tellers supporting me."

Within days, David had severed two managers, taken the reins, and created a short video summarizing his decision and process for his tiger team.

What David realized through this process was that he was at the center of the vision for the future of Avid. "As the founder, I embody the DNA of the mission and direction like no one else. I exude that, and I create opportunities for others by holding that so rightly and clearly within me," he shares. "I am also uniquely positioned to enroll those around me in the vision with my enthusiasm for the vision."

HOW TO SELECT YOUR PERSONAL BOARD OF DIRECTORS

The process of assembling a personal board of directors might seem daunting at first. Here are a few tips to make this process more accessible:

+ Get clear on your intent and the extent of your ask. Your personal board of directors might be a group you rely on for years or for just one inflection point.
+ Decide on your target size. Your personal board of directors

might be as small as one person or as large as ten. One or more people might come in or step away at any given time.

+ Choose whom to ask from your network:
  » Pick people who could be most helpful to you, even if asking feels uncomfortable. If you don't feel at all uncomfortable, you likely haven't started at the top of your wish list.
  » Pick people whom you trust and respect. These people are honest, and when they speak honestly to you, you believe they have your best interests at heart.
  » Pick people who have domain expertise in the topic you want your board to discuss: a job pivot, a new solopreneur business, or a new target sales market.
  » Pick people you like. If you (and they) are going to spend discretionary time together, make it enjoyable.
  » Pick people who understand you and your motivations. You're looking for insights specifically tied to what drives you.

HOW (AND WHEN) TO USE
YOUR PERSONAL BOARD OF ADVISORS

The next five chapters of this book might inform your outline for your inaugural personal board of directors meeting or your strategy for how and when to convene that board. When you have decided to gather a group, use the following exercise to solidify your intent, process, and goals for your assembly.

=== **EXERCISE** ===

Organize Your Inaugural Personal Board of Directors Meeting

+ Who's coming?
+ Prework (for you or them)
+ Your draft agenda
+ Questions you'll ask
+ Outcomes you're seeking

- Elements of your action plan that you'll complete within one week (or one month) of your board of directors meeting
- Accountability requests that you wish to make of your board
- Plan for follow-up to your board. Let them know how you're incorporating what you learned
- Plan for securing subsequent feedback on your process from your board
- Plan to return the kindness. Go beyond asking "How can I help you?" Find out what interests them and find ways to add value over time.

CHAPTER 8

YOUR TWO-MINUTE BIO

As I've shared, the philosophy underlying the sales strategy of passionate ambivalence and never asking for the sale starts with you. Let's dive into how you present yourself. You likely have introduced yourself thousands of times. If you're in a business where you are a central part of the offering, you're likely introducing yourself all the time. In any aspect of your life associated with selling you, the most seemingly inconsequential introduction can prove to be important.

But what you may not realize is that the way you introduce yourself is a key component of selling. If you are a solopreneur or your current pursuit relates directly to selling or marketing something, you will always be selling.

You might find yourself at a fold-up table showcasing Girl Scout cookies, your first job interview as a restaurant dishwasher, a meeting of a faith-based youth group, an ice-breaking session during counselor training before the kids arrive at camp, a sorority rush, dinner with the parents of your new squeeze, a parent-teacher conference for your third grader, a new book club, or myriad other situations in which you will be called upon to perform a one- or two-minute self-introduction.

Every one of these scenes is preparation and reinforcement for generating a core short-form bio that you can tweak based on the needs of the moment. I want to focus on the version of your bio that you will use when you indirectly or directly sell yourself in a professional context or in the context of pitching your solopreneur business. When will that be? you ask. Every single introduction, starting now. So let's get this right.

BUILDING YOUR BIO

When I think about the value of a bio, I think about my favorite Steve Jobs quotation: "You can't connect the dots looking forward; you can only connect them looking backwards. So you have to trust that the dots will somehow connect in your future. You have to trust in something—your gut, destiny, life, karma, whatever. This approach has never let me down, and it has made all the difference in my life."[5]

Whenever I am working with someone on their bio, I walk them through this exercise or encourage them to do it on their own and to revisit it every year or two.

> **Step One:** Get loose, limber, and spacious in your mind (and body, if you like). I don't have any formula for how to do this, but taking a few deep breaths in your desk chair, doing a yoga pose or two, eating a square of dark chocolate (always a great idea), or taking a walk around the block will do just fine.

> **Step Two:** Grab a sheet or two of paper. If you are wedded to working only on a digital screen, that's fine. I love the feeling of pen and paper for more creative exercises, but you do you. No matter what, turn off digital notifications if you can.

> **Step Three:** Take five minutes and draft your one- to two-minute biography. For guidance, ninety seconds of speaking is about two hundred words.

> **Step Four:** After you feel comfortable with a solid draft, read it aloud with a timer to confirm that it is no shorter than thirty seconds and no longer than two minutes when read at a normal pace.

> **Step Five:** When you read your draft bio out loud, you might notice things that don't sound like anything you would ever say. That's

---

5   "'You've Got to Find What You Love,' Jobs Says," Stanford Report, June 12, 2005.

great awareness. Rewrite those phrases so they sound like you, and be sure they sound like you on a good day with a reasonable amount of confidence and conviction.

Step Six: Go back to what you've just written (and spoken) and underline or highlight all the places where you think you were intentionally or incidentally selling. These places may be subtle. One way to pick up on these is to imagine that you are listening to someone else read the bio you've just penned for yourself. What might you notice? What bits did you include that spark interest or set you apart? I recently introduced a new college graduate to a CEO who might have a role that's a good fit. When I wrote what amounted to a short bio in that email (to which the graduate's résumé was attached), I highlighted the fact that this young man had served as the captain of his high school and college club gymnastics teams for a total of four years. I mentioned that he had grown the collegiate team by 50 percent during his time there. By sharing this—something different from a big-time college brand or a grade point average—I meant to spotlight this individual's leadership, commitment, and followership. I was selling, implying that this young man had a history of rising to leadership based on the sentiments of his peers. I love this quality in people, and I think it portends success in many business roles.

Step Seven: For each spot that you just highlighted in your draft bio, make a note of what you think you were implying and how you think that articulates a selling point about you. There are so many ways you might build selling into your bio, as I've suggested. To get your juices flowing and your radar calibrated for this, I'll suggest thirteen that I particularly like. My list surely has my bias in it, so check for things that are relevant in your line of work and for you:

1. You showed a pattern of increasing responsibility.
2. You exhibited dedication to pushing through challenging circumstances.

3. You stood out as unique, capable, or superb.
4. You displayed creativity.
5. You were authentic and even vulnerable (in a way that created potential risk to you).
6. You were scrappy or tenacious, overcoming tough odds or making a lot with a little.
7. You were charming, deft, kind, or persuasive in relationships with others.
8. You were a stellar manager or influencer of people; people followed you from one team or job to another because they wanted to work for or with you.
9. You showed leadership whether it was requested or not.
10. You won!
11. You lost and learned something!
12. You showed humility without compromising your sense of yourself.
13. You demonstrated how passionate you are about your reasons for doing your work.

It can be useful to run your bio by someone who loves you enough to be a great ally in helping you stand for you. Ask them what they heard. Ask them what you missed.

Step Eight: Finally, ask yourself this question: "On a scale from 1 to 10, how likely would I be to want to learn more about a business run by the person with that bio if I had a need or want the person might serve?"

If your answer is 8 or lower, keep reading, refining, and seeking feedback. If your answer is 9 or 10, you still might learn a few things over time in a story that will be constantly evolving, but well done!

A BREAKDOWN OF A TWO-MINUTE BIO

Now you get a break from self-inquiry. I'm going to share *my* two-minute bio. I share way less at a dinner party, and I cut about half of this in any social situation, but this is a reliable go-to for me:

> I decided I wanted to be a federal prosecutor with the US Department of Justice when I was eleven. Twenty years later, I was. My job as a trial attorney in the Civil Rights Division was a match for all of me.
>
> But in 1998, I was lit up about the potential of the Internet. I decided to start an e-commerce business focused on baby products as a side hustle. I had no baby, had no business experience, and knew nothing about tech, but I made it work. My passion for business eclipsed my love of law. I interviewed for two "real" business jobs at companies and got one, a sales role at what is now Warner Bros. Discovery.
>
> After four years, I realized I was too rebellious for a large company, and I spent the next decade in C-level roles in tech startups. I raised some venture money. Some companies worked and successfully sold; some didn't. Along the way, I cofounded a VC fund that invested in startups with at least one woman in leadership.
>
> Twelve years ago, I did a coaching session with Kaley Klemp. That day changed my life. Her work, Conscious Leadership, helped me see that my key pattern of intensity had fueled much of my success, but it also was creating a ceiling for my personal and professional growth. I learned that intensity was only one of many leadership strategies. This breakthrough gave me more access to love, joy, ease, and creativity at work. As I learned it, I taught conscious leadership at the companies I led.
>
> Ten years ago, I became a full-time conscious leadership coach and facilitator. I draw on my experiences as a tech operator to help talented leaders and teams reach their potential.

How did you feel about my bio? How would you rate it on the same scale I asked you to use for your own?

I will repeat my bio with a markup as follows that shows the places where I think I'm softly selling. Everything I am saying here is subjective. You may disagree with me on what is and isn't a selling point. That is important. I do not recommend that your bio be a fit for everyone. You want to highlight things that make you a great fit for people with whom you want to work (or whom you want to befriend, etc.). Use my bio as an illustration of how to do this informal selling. Then craft your bio to include things that you value in your backstory.

I decided I wanted to be a federal prosecutor with the US Department of Justice when I was eleven. Twenty years later, I was.

Here I illustrate conviction about what I want to achieve and a willingness to achieve over a long period of time, doing a thing most people respect.

My job as a trial attorney in the Civil Rights Division was a match for all of me.

Civil rights may be controversial as a point of view, but I'm sharing something personal about myself that really matters. In truth, it's not optimal for me to work with clients who aren't aligned with my values, so I'm signaling my commitment to people I would want to work with.

But in 1998, I was lit up about the potential of the Internet. I decided to start an e-commerce business focused on baby products as a side hustle.

I got involved in the Internet at the very beginning. On one hand, this makes me old, and that's not super in the minds of some people. On the other hand, it shows that I pay attention to current, meaningful trends and that I found a way to get involved as an early mover. I was fearless. This also shows that I work hard—I had a day job and a night job.

I had no baby, had no business experience, and knew nothing about tech, but I made it work. My passion for business eclipsed my love of law.

I am not afraid of doing things that are new to me and diving in and building expertise from zero to one. I am passionate about things. I am willing to question long-held beliefs about my purpose and stay present to shifts in what I most want out of life. In this deliberate way, I followed my heart.

I interviewed for two "real" business jobs at companies and got one, a sales role at what is now Warner Bros. Discovery.

I got one offer from two interviews. I'm desirable and compelling. That job was with a company many people have heard of. I also got a real job title with very little business experience.

After four years, I realized I was too rebellious for a large company, and I spent the next decade in C-level roles in tech startups. I raised some venture money. Some companies worked and successfully sold; some didn't.

I am rebellious. This is true. It's not for everyone, but it must be acceptable—desirable, even—to anyone I work with. I pivoted with ease from a big company to small companies, and I made my way from director to C-level roles in a new context. I raised venture money and sold a company or two, which count as markers of success in the startup sector where I spend most of my time. I am also humble enough to tell you I had failures, and I tell you that I had some success. And I'm promoting my affinity for exactly the kinds of companies I want to work with.

Along the way, I cofounded a VC fund that invested in startups with at least one woman in leadership.

I did another thing that shows expansion in a space (startups) to a position of greater authority (an investor). I raised money in a different context. I had a mission that I cared about and made a difference there.

Twelve years ago, I did a coaching session with Kaley Klemp. That day changed my life. She helped me see that my key pattern of intensity had fueled much of my success, but it also was creating a ceiling for my personal and professional growth. I learned that intensity was only one of many leadership strategies. This breakthrough gave me more access to love, joy, ease, and creativity at work. As I learned it, I taught conscious leadership at the companies I led.

I arrived at the work I do through a very personal access point. I worked directly with one of the global leaders and authors in the work that I practice. This work changed my life, and that's why I'm so committed to doing it more. I'm forceful while being a generous person.

Ten years ago, I became a full-time conscious leadership coach and facilitator. I draw on my experiences as a tech operator to help talented leaders and teams reach their potential.

I took another big risk to commit myself fully to the work I'm talking to you about. I probably have made it work because I'm talking to you, and you might have heard about the game-changing work I did with a company or leader you admire.

I ran this two-minute bio by one of the workshops I conducted as I was preparing to write this book. Participants found it vulnerable and accurate. One notable piece of feedback someone shared was that the bio was stealthy. It felt like I was just listing a series of facts, but I was weaving a sales pitch. Another commented on the storytelling and emotional connection. I think all those features are key to building a great bio that drives sales of a business that depends heavily on you.

I did not write this version of my biography at age twenty-two. I have been writing it all along. I refine it as I do more, change something, or learn something about what seems to be working and not working when I share it. Give yourself the same grace.

AUTHENTICITY AND THE BIO

Bios are a fitting time to think about authenticity and how it plays into selling from the starting point of you. My friend Leah coined the concept of Suemanship as a playful way to spot my occasional bouts of hyperbole and my seemingly unconscious tendency to sell. There's a tongue-in-cheek implication that there may be a little, shall we say, added enthusiasm attached to how I sell. I'm careful to always be honest. But this bio is not a complete recitation of everything I've ever done. It's selective. Yours should be, too.

When I think about how my enthusiasm, energy, and quasi-myopic point of view merge, I think most of my selling is 90 percent authentic with a 10 percent sizzle factor. That 10 percent comes in selection and storytelling.

For example, I use a pithy phrase to talk about my last executive role: "Ten years ago, I became a full-time conscious leadership coach and facilitator." Like many pithy phrases, this one glosses over what really happened. I was the chief revenue officer of a tech company that sold software to small businesses. I started that job in the summer and won the "most valuable team member" award at the holiday party that year. Three months later, late on a Sunday night, I received an email from my boss and CEO saying he had "lost confidence" in me. I remember where I was when I saw that email. I remember how hard I cried. I remember feeling like I'd just received the most targeted gut punch I had never imagined. I gathered myself, showed up at work the next day, and scheduled a 1:1 with my boss. We agreed that day would be my last day. There are myriad reasons for how and why that happened. I received some severance that gave me a couple of months to come up with a new plan, and my current profession became that plan. I don't talk about this in my bio, even though thinking about that night still hurts.

ASPIRATIONAL, NOT DECEPTIVE, STORYTELLING

To build a strong bio or a successful business revolving around you, quality storytelling is a must.

One important aspect of your story might be including in your bio not just what you *have done* but what you want to do. Your bio may include aspirational features and still be honest. If you are currently selling software to middle-market companies or small businesses, but you *want* to be selling similar software to enterprise customers, you might include a phrase such as "I'm currently an account executive focused on small and midsize businesses, and I'm building up my skill set to one day lead an enterprise selling team doing seven-figure sales deals." This isn't deceptive; it's visionary. Placing yourself in the context of where you are and where you're headed can be an inspiring aspect of your bio. It may offer others signals of how they can choose to be a part of driving your current and future success.

Here is a great example of a visionary two-minute bio. My friend and former client Heather Frick wrote this as she was transitioning from a role as a tech executive to executive coaching as a side hustle:

Heather Frick is an executive coach for high achievers who are ready to play bigger. Sure, she can help you be a better leader. But being a better leader isn't good enough for Heather, and it shouldn't be good enough for you, either. Still reading? You and Heather might be a great fit. Heather helps performers become winners and winners become iconic. As the former CMO of Assent and a powerhouse at Oracle, Heather knows what it takes to drive massive growth, lead major transformations, and build cultures that win. She's partnered with top leadership at brands like Nordstrom, Levi's, Dell, and Verizon, guiding them through high-stakes growth and digital transformations, and now she's coaching execs at companies like Microsoft, Adobe, Capital One, and Shopify to do the same.

Heather's approach? Fierce, focused, and full of heart. She's a former Division I athlete, so she knows how to turn playful competition into fuel, and her coaching blends that edge with practical conscious leadership tools to keep you thriving in fast-paced, high-pressure environments. Based in Colorado, Heather's all about wellness, adventure, and bringing her whole self to everything she does. So, are you a winner in waiting? Heather may be the coach you have been looking for.

What I appreciate here is how well this story conveys Heather's energy and spirit. It sets an aspirational tone for her and her prospects. She qualifies herself with recognized client brands and her background as a C-level executive. My favorite part of this bio is Heather's reference to her history as a Division I athlete. As I mentioned, I have always loved hiring athletes. I have a story that they are tenacious, team-oriented, fun, and gritty. Heather is all these things, and her bio surreptitiously messages those qualities and values to her prospects.

OPTIMIZING THE HUMILITY-TO-VISIONARY RATIO

If Heather's coaching bio or this entire chapter threatened your core value of humility, I see you. You likely will notice in this book that I often use humility as a selling device. Well-placed understatement drives high interest and engagement. That said, rote humility, especially to the extent that your bio radically understates what you've done and what you do, will not serve you. Be honest and be comfortable. That's critical to selling you. Find a way that you can communicate how you're superb so that others can see it without knowing you for ten years or interviewing all your best friends, clients, and middle school teachers.

A good tool for analyzing where your two-minute bio falls on the humility continuum is to run it by five good friends and colleagues whom you trust. Share your bio and ask them these questions:

+ How did you feel reading this? Name one or two feelings.
+ How does this bio affect your trust in me? Positively or negatively?
+ Does this bio feel false or unpleasantly arrogant to you? If so, where? What could I say that would be truer?
+ Would you hire me to do the thing you know I want to do based on this bio? If yes, why? If no, why?
+ What is one change you want me to make here for any reason?

Once you secure this feedback, you will have a sense of whether you've struck the right chord in terms of authenticity, confidence, and the absence of overselling or desperation. That gut check is important.

THE ELEVATOR INTRO

Before we leave the topic of your personal introduction, let's turn our attention to a scenario that is more common than the one that might call for your two-minute bio. This is the five-second response to any version of the question "What do you do?" I want to pause here to note all the feelings you may have about being asked this question. You may hate it. You may agree with my close friend who despises this question because she sees it as a quick way for people to "rank" each other at cocktail parties. You may never ask this question. Frankly, let's shelve the "why" questions about this question and just acknowledge that you will be asked this question hundreds of times a year.

I strongly suggest that you formulate a great answer. Everyone you meet is a potential lead or a potential referrer to a lead. I'm not suggesting that you hard sell in either the two-minute bio or this five-second answer, but I want your response to be solid and intriguing enough that a reasonable conversationalist might generously toss back a follow-up question.

I was particularly hamstrung by this question for years after founding my coaching company. I answered this question offhandedly and so humbly that there was no chance anyone would have *any idea* of what I actually did for a living. I was potentially ripping them off from getting to know me (if that is what they were trying to do), and I was surely ripping myself off by hiding behind a flip response about one of the most important things in my life.

Once I realized that and how often I was doing this, I woke up. I noticed that I had some shame around being an executive coach. I live in a place where 80 percent of the people at the gym on a given day might be executive coaches. This was likely a limiting belief. I also saw that if I were more honest about what I really do for a living, it might sound incredibly arrogant. My worry about arrogance rings of an upper limit. My more conscious statement about what I do went something like

I have the privilege of building intimate relationships with many people and businesses that have a meaningful impact on innovation and our economy. I am close enough to them that I have permission to challenge them in hopes we will learn as much as we can from each other.

That seems ridiculously cocky, and it's also way longer than five seconds. Once I had the awareness of what I was up to in this pattern—choosing between playing small and imagining that the only alternative was loquacious bombast—I settled in the middle. Here's what I say now:

I'm a conscious leadership coach and facilitator to innovative tech companies and the people who lead them.

Once you develop your two-minute and five-second bios, I recommend that you get very good at presenting them appropriately in context. If your body betrays you, if you shrink back in your seat as you begin introducing yourself, your hard work here will be for naught. You will spend time building these bios. Practice bringing all of you—your tone, spirit, and physical presence—to the moments when you share them. I have a few tips to help you get this right ahead of time and in the moment:

+ As I shared earlier, practice your two-minute and five-second bios with friends, family, and anyone who wants to see you succeed. Ask for their candid feedback.
+ When you are called upon to share one of your bios, take a deep breath and reset your posture and eye contact before you start.
+ During an occasion when you and others are doing introductions, notice if your imposter voice is talking to you inside your head. She may say, "Oh, that person is more impressive than you." Or "Golly, you look underdressed." Try to breathe through any messages you're getting in the buckets of comparison or self-criticism. In your mind, look at those thoughts or that imposter voice and say (silently), "Back off. I will come back to you later, but for now, these people want to meet me, not you."

At an event recently, an organizer stepped onstage to introduce the next speaker. He was dressed perfectly in a purple velvet jacket just right for the formal informality of this event. When he began introducing himself, he paused and said, "I have been told that I generally move too quickly when I'm introducing myself, I think because I don't like being the center of attention.

But I've received this feedback, and I'm going to slow down." And he did. And it was relaxing, informative, genuine, and warm. Those are exactly the adjectives I would use to describe him.

Now it's your turn.

EXERCISE
Return, Revise, and Revisit

Using the examples and tips in this chapter, return to your two-minute bio and revise it as much or as little as you like. Then draft a new five-second answer to the question "What do you do?"

CHAPTER 9

FROM WHO YOU'VE BEEN TO WHO YOU ARE

Your Core Values

Once you have firmed up your two-minute bio, I recommend that you nail down your core values. In *Dare to Lead*, Brené Brown defines values as the principles or beliefs we hold about ourselves and human behavior. She says our values often dictate how we spend our time, money, and energy. Yes, it is possible to engage in a core values exercise as a pro forma waste of time, generating a few words for a proverbial plaque above your desk.

Don't let that happen. Instead, treat this as a deep inquiry into who you are and how you want to show up in your business. Choosing your core values—thinking through the subtle delineations between those values that centrally define you and those that, though lovely, are merely peripheral—will help you better know and articulate what it is like to work with you. Knowing your values will also help you choose clients and projects and will help you decide to sever clients and engagements when a core value is no longer being served or has been breached.

Here are my top five current core values:

1. Authenticity
2. Courage
3. Dynamism

4. Humor
5. Love

In *Dare to Lead*, Brown also advocates for drilling down to choose your top two core values. I like this extra step for the additional clarity it provides, despite the challenge of choosing just two of my precious top five. Here they are for me:

1. Courage
2. Dynamism

Courage incorporates my version of authenticity, the willingness to speak directly to power, the affection I have for creating finely tuned, constant feedback mechanisms between an individual executive client and me or among a team of executives. I routinely say, and am told, that I offer challenges to others with love seemingly as the core motivation. When I am authentic, I am sometimes incredibly open and vulnerable, sometimes incisively direct, and sometimes both. I am willing to speak and be wrong. I am willing to form gut-level instincts, hold them loosely, and share them with a present awareness that I can miss the mark. I create conversations and relationships that are characterized by courage on all sides. With colleagues, clients, family, friends, and romantic partners, I stay current on the things that are upsetting or delighting me.

When I sell myself, I sell with courage. I will talk more about that later in this book. For now, know that I take risks in every area of sales, from reaching out to prospects who may be perfect to pricing aggressively to saying no to extensive sales and invoicing processes like scope-of-work documents and detailed proposals. Passionate ambivalence requires courage. A mindset of passionate ambivalence also *generates* courage. As we let go of fear during a sales effort or any type of performance and fully focus on the task at hand, we become more courageous. The detachment associated with ambivalence removes fear and engenders courage. Don't worry; you can learn how to do this, even if courage is not one of your two core values.

Dynamism incorporates my love of change, my natural affinity for improvisation, my creative mind, and my ability to bring new ideas to life quickly and effortlessly. In my mind, I am stretchy and elastic. I launch new programs, put them out into the market, and take them right back if I see that my approach, my timing, or the offering itself is not in demand. I fail fast. When I get tough feedback, I often feel a sting and begin to get defensive at the first pass. Then, after a few moments, I come back to presence, eager to learn (or at least open to learning) from the message I just received. When I feel an emotion, I allow myself to *fully feel it*. I cry all the time in client meetings with C-level leaders. Candidly, this book is too short to list all the places I've cried. Ask my partner, who routinely refers to my "daily cry." Things that are said can be magical or painful or just true, and I feel them, allow them in my system, and then move on.

When I sell myself, I sell with dynamism. I am committed to showing prospects in a first conversation what the experience of working with me is like. I listen carefully, and I respond in the moment anytime I either think I might be helpful, I might show that person what it's like to work with me, or both. I don't rehearse. I don't use scripts. I don't do what I have heard some consultants do and hold back an insight that might be useful for a time when a prospect is paying me. I use very loose agendas for almost everything, and I endeavor to be present in the moment when I'm selling.

As I write this, the hero image copy on my business site at HeySue.com reads, "Fearlessly Authentic: From speaking to consulting to coaching leaders, Sue delivers. She is real. Vulnerable. Incisive. Funny. Challenging." I probably should change "incisive" to "dynamic." Because I'm dynamic, I may go do that right now.

I use these top two values to answer these questions during different phases of my business and sales motions:

+ Is this client someone who feels energetically aligned? Are they courageous or dynamic?
+ Does this gig call for my courage or dynamism? If not, should I let it go?
+ Is my two-minute bio showcasing me as courageous and dynamic? If not, let's look again.
+ When a prospect asks me what I am like, do I proudly and credibly say I am courageous and dynamic?

- Does my website—imagery and copy—suggest courage and dynamism?
- Are the types of work in which I'm engaging courageous and dynamic?
- How could I be braver or more dynamic today?
- In a call with a prospective client, did I show up as courageous and dynamic?
- When I read the feedback about my last project, did anyone mention that I was courageous or dynamic? If not, why not?
- Are my top two core values of courage and dynamism current? Are they still at the heart of everything I want and do? If not, I want to revisit my top two.

Once you choose your top two values, I encourage you to ask these questions of yourself regularly. When you notice areas of misalignment with your values, actively interrogate the rationale for the disconnect. You may notice that you want to pivot your values or that you want to pivot your work, your way of working, your client base, or something else.

One of my favorite examples of selling and business building from a place of extreme values alignment is a MergeLane portfolio company. As I've shared, the concepts in this book apply to sellers of any type. They also apply to startup founders who are selling their vision—and, in this case, physical products—to a market.

Naomi Gonzalez and Fran Dunaway, Cofounders, TomboyX

In 2013, Fran Dunaway and Naomi Gonzalez cofounded TomboyX, an underwear and apparel company primarily targeting the then underserved LGBTQ community.

For the next ten years, TomboyX influenced, if not created, the market. The cofounders did that by placing themselves at the center of their brand, and investors, journalists, and consumers swooned. Not only did TomboyX essentially invent a category of undergarments and swimsuits for an audience that had been invisible to apparel manufacturers, but it also went from niche to mainstream at pace.

I met Fran and Naomi when they applied for a slot in the MergeLane accelerator program in 2014. My investment partner and I knew that the odds were against any apparel company earning venture-scale returns, but once we were on a video call with these two founders, feeling the depth of their passion and commitment to supplying underwear and other apparel primarily to the LGBTQ audience, we were sold. We loved their energy and vision. We elected to invest, convinced that they could defy the odds if anyone could.

Fran and Naomi had backgrounds in television and politics. "We didn't know a P&L from a balance sheet," says Fran. "Neither of us had come from the apparel industry. We were a married lesbian couple, but we knew that there was white space out there because we were part of that white space."

They launched a Kickstarter campaign for their nascent company early on and raised $76,000 in thirty days. They started doing their own limited manufacturing runs of shirts, and they put the TomboyX logo on curated merchandise made by others to get their start. "We looked at our data and realized we were selling a lot of underwear that we weren't making," says Fran. "It was a bit like 'tighty whitey' briefs but in colors. They weren't very comfortable, and the size range was narrow, but there was one pair in every online order." They began getting requests for boxer briefs for women, and they saw that there was nothing like that on the market. "We found a talented product developer who understood us, and we asked her to make comfortable boxer briefs for women from size XS to 4X at the same price point. Our product leader told us that's not how it's done, and we said we didn't care. So she did it."

Eighteen months after the Kickstarter campaign, TomboyX launched the first boxer briefs for women. "We weren't sure how we were gonna pay for the pallet we ordered, so we did a presale campaign," says Fran. "The first order of boxer briefs sold out before they arrived. At that point, TomboyX became an underwear company.

"Honestly, the two of us were not what we would consider very strong capitalists at the time," says Fran. "We had always been in purpose-driven careers, so it didn't sit right to just make something for the sake of making money. It was important to us that we made sure our values were imbued in the company from the beginning. That meant quality, sustainability, community, inclusion, representation, and a focus on our team members."

"Everything we did emanated from our values," says Naomi.

I learned quickly how committed Fran and Naomi were to those values when I suggested in 2015 that they broaden their focus to all women who regarded themselves as "tomboys," meaning a potentially broader audience than people who identified as LGBTQ. Sure, as a tomboy from a young age myself, I was projecting a bit in my ask, but Fran and Naomi were clear. They believed their audience was more specific (at least at the outset), and that audience was large enough to form the basis for a large company. They visibly adhered to this commitment long before it was cool. "We were the first ones out there that had trans models," says Fran. "We had plus sizes from the very beginning. We had diversity in gender and the BIPOC community. And we've always offered styles that were all at the same price, which was hard to find. We wanted to celebrate people just as they were. We weren't telling them how to be cool. We assumed they were cool, and we wanted to celebrate that with them."

"I think the biggest challenge and opportunity was that we were on the cutting edge of redefining what sexy is," says Naomi. "Male investors would say their girlfriends wouldn't wear our stuff because it wasn't sexy. We believed that sexy is whatever makes you feel sexy. And it comes from loving yourself, really and truly. But at first, it wasn't an easy sell. And that's what we were up against. We talked to a lot of women that didn't get it, either. It was an uphill climb for us. But we look at the market today, and almost every brand of women's underwear markets boxer briefs."

"Our audience grew well beyond our initial aspirations," says Fran. "A lot of people looked at us and thought we were a lesbian underwear company. But we had become a comfortable underwear company for everyone.

"Our 2022 launch at Target as a centerpiece to the store's nationwide Pride collection was our true mic-drop moment. To know that there were kids and people that were walking into a Target and seeing themselves represented was magical."

Target invited Fran and Naomi to a photo shoot for the line. "It was incredible," says Naomi. "Target made sure that the crew filming the shoot for the ads was either queer or queer ally. They had trans models. People on the set were crying because they felt like they could truly be themselves. They were so proud to be working with Target, and they were thrilled that Target had chosen a brand like TomboyX to collaborate with because we were and are the real thing. It wasn't a PR stunt. It was a real collaboration. And it mattered. It mattered to many people. And for us, that was a big deal."

EXERCISE
Identify Your Core Values

Here is a list of possible core values.

Accomplishment	Grace	Persuasion
Action	Gratitude	Planning
Adventure	Growth	Play
Agency	Happiness	Power
Agility	Health	Pride
Art	Home	Relationship
Beauty	Hope	Resilience
Challenge	Humor	Respect
Change	Independence	Risk
Community	Inner peace	Safety
Connection	Inner strength	Security
Consistency	Inspiration	Self-control
Control	Integrity	Self-expression
Courage	Intellect	Self-respect
Creativity	Intuition	Serenity
Dependability	Invention	Service
Dignity	Justice	Spirituality
Empathy	Kindness	Spontaneity
Encouragement	Laughter	Structure
Enlightenment	Leadership	Support
Excellence	Learning	Tenacity
Fairness	Love	Tradition
Family	Loyalty	Trust
Feelings	Nature	Understanding
Flexibility	Openness	Wealth
Freedom	Partnership	Winning
Friendship	Passion	Wisdom
Fun	Patience	Work

If values that you hold are not included in this list, they are still viable.

+ Choose your top ten values.
+ Narrow your list of ten to five. Think through your definitions, prioritization, and rationale for this cut.
+ Do one final cut to your top two values. Think through your definitions, prioritization, and rationale for this cut.
+ Then look at your LinkedIn profile, your website, your other marketing materials, your sales pitch, and how you talk about your business at cocktail parties. If you find an incongruity, find a way to resolve it amicably and sustainably.

CHAPTER 10

HOW YOU SHOW UP

Your Essence Qualities, Personas, and Personality Type

W e've nailed the two-minute bio, five-second pitch, and core values. The next step in understanding the you whom you plan to sell is to understand the features of you that will reliably show up as you do work that depends heavily on you.

ESSENCE QUALITIES

In my training to be a conscious leadership coach, I learned about the concept of an "essence quality" as distinguished from a personality trait. An essence quality is an aspect of you that reliably shows up when you enter the room. It is a quality you love about yourself. Other people likely love these qualities in you, too. If we were to ask your closest friends and family members to name one or two persistent aspects of you, they would point to an essence quality or two. Essence qualities are fundamental, indispensable, reliable, constant. They cross boundaries between your personal and professional life. Your essence qualities may be tightly connected to your top core values.

I frequently ask people to name one of their essence qualities. It's my favorite icebreaker. Sometimes someone will say, "An essence quality of mine is sarcasm!" I will push back by asking, "Do you really love sarcasm as a quality of yours?" and they will most often say no. I will ask again, and they will often mention humor as a true essence quality. People don't supply a true essence quality in a sentence that ends in a question mark or an exclamation point. It's usually quiet, continuous, and solid.

An essence quality of mine is fearlessness. It's not that I'm free of fear, but in situations that feel risky, I will generally choose the more challenging path because my desire for connection and love generally outweighs my fear of rejection or loneliness. I am game to engage in conversations that may promote conflict. I'm eager to skip the small talk to get to the crux of an issue. I don't give (or enjoy receiving) "feedback sandwiches" containing a positive comment, a critical comment, and then a positive comment. Behaviors like that feel false to me. I prefer the more direct path, even if it is sometimes scary.

Friends of mine have essence qualities including humor, reliability, get-shit-done, playfulness, love, tenderness, storytelling, curiosity, vision, helpfulness, creativity, love of learning, exploration, and ease. Knowing one or two of your essence qualities can be helpful in assessing whether the work you do and the clients you choose allow you to work close to your essence qualities.

Take a moment and reflect on two or three of your essence qualities. Be sure these are aspects of yourself that you love. As you reflect on them in your mind or jot them in a journal, do your best to own them instead of shaking them off with self-deprecation.

PERSONALITY AND PERSONAS

Although essence qualities are constant, most of us also carry around personalities. Personalities are traits, behaviors, or roles that we bring out—consciously or unconsciously—in response to a situation. In some cases, a personality trait may be related to an essence quality. For example, my fearlessness is an essence quality, but my brashness (a less-than-delightful extension of fearlessness) is a trait. My personality traits also include being direct, forceful, sycophantic, challenging, egomaniacal, intense, controlling, insecure, and urgent. These are all varieties of intensity.

When I am not at my best, my personality traits often show up, sometimes in the form of "personas." Those personas might appear in stressful moments. If I'm not paying attention, I won't notice when they take the helm. It's good to check in on the presence of personas when you're slightly unsettled, on edge, or in an old, familiar setting. For example, I notice that I take on a range of personas the moment I cross the threshold of my mother's home. Sometimes I act like a child, wanting her to take care of basic needs like having food in the fridge. Sometimes my inner sixteen-year-old rebel shows up to engage in conflict with her. Sometimes I'm in my essence qualities, lovingly appreciating her and the warm relationship we crafted long after I left home.

As another example, when I walk into a cocktail party, which is not my favorite setting, I often show up as a persona who is pithy, funny, and hoping to be liked. If I get tired of small talk, I might pivot to an intense persona who asks deep questions in hopes of rescuing my impatient self from the sheer pablum of most parties. Sometimes my personality traits or personas serve me. Sometimes they undermine me. I like being familiar with the range because my awareness often brings me back to presence and a mindset that is closer to my more lovable essence qualities.

I recommend becoming familiar with your essence qualities and the sometimes related personality traits or personas. This is helpful for sellers who are selling themselves, as it helps them understand more fully how they show up in the sales process. It may also help sellers understand how and whether to work with prospective clients with various personality traits.

Personality traits often affect how someone feels about the idea of selling. In one workshop I ran, an attendee I'll call Melissa said she hated selling. At the time, Melissa was an operations executive in a technology company, and she was considering leaving her full-time role to start a solopreneur consulting business. She had already done a few side hustles as a consultant; in all those instances, it seemed that her clients had metaphorically forced the door down to work with her. I asked Melissa what she hated about sales, and she said, "I feel like I'm trying to get people to do something they don't want to do. Or that they're going to think I'm only being nice to them or only connecting with them to get something out of them."

Melissa had beliefs, ingrained in her personality, about what it means to "sell," including the idea that selling involves manipulating people to do something they might not want to do. I hope to dispel that idea here. I talked more with Melissa, and she acknowledged that part of her personality, one of her dominant personas, is wanting to be liked. She felt that selling to people involved creating a transactional connection that would undermine her wish to be seen as likable. For Melissa to become an effective seller in a business based predominantly on her, I recommended that she look at her beliefs around selling and how those beliefs intersect with her wants and traits and her ideal approach to sales.

Here are some representative selling personas I have heard in myself or others:

- **Peep:** This persona wants to be shy. They want to respond only to direct questions, and they don't want to be too aggressive in the sales process for fear of alienating prospects or clients.
- **Deets:** This persona wants to sell primarily with data and extreme detail. They believe anything worth buying can be proved through data, and if a conversation strays into an area of what a prospect or client might want—emotionally or philosophically— this persona brings it all back to a spreadsheet to stay on safe and trusted ground.
- **Greatest Showman:** This persona loves big conferences and trade shows, where they can gladhand and buy rounds of drinks after the workday for large groups, some of whom may be prospects. They are magnetic, a big personality whom everyone wants to get to know.
- **Bully:** This persona applies pressure in sales, believing that a hard-driving sale is the way to get it done. They may use fear tactics with prospects, sounding an alarm like "What is your boss going to think if you're the only company not using our product?" They press even harder at the end of the quarter or the fiscal year because they want to make or beat quota.
- **Mr. Pound:** This persona has been schooled in the science of hammering a message as hard as they can. They believe that

no ad, email, or LinkedIn post gets any attention until it's been seen five times a day, and they're relentless about ensuring that the message gets out about a person's business offering. Visibility makes sales happen!

+ **BFF:** This persona makes it their business to know and remember every aspect of an important prospect's life. They send flowers on birthdays, check in on kids' milestones, and perhaps enable venting sessions with prospects to show how much they really care.

+ **Woe:** This persona is having a really hard time making sales, and they want the prospects they know best to help them out at a difficult time by getting a contract across the line. Woe brings a lot of victim energy to the sales conversation.

+ **Mercenary:** This persona is all about the money. They know that what they are selling is highly consultative, but hey, time is money, and there's just not enough time to be too consultative in a selling process or all the value will be given away. Mercenary believes that old saw that no one will buy the cow if the milk is free. They live by that one.

+ **Daisy:** Daisy hates talking or thinking about money. Money talk feels base and almost dirty to them. They would rather talk about spiritual, beautiful ideas. Daisy and Mercenary really do not get along. Daisy might be a persona of someone who *also* has Mercenary as a persona, and that internal discussion goes something like this:

Daisy: Oh, I really like this prospect. I agree with their values. We should cut our rates by 70 percent because they are working on something so valuable to society.

Mercenary: OMG. Who let *you* into this conversation? Don't you know we have bills to pay, kids' college to plan for, and a deep desire to one day be able to afford NHL season tickets? We work for *money*, baby!

Armed with these persona examples, you can see that personas feel extreme. They generally are extreme examples, a personality trait that is "in charge," running a process without a check from another persona or you. I endeavored to list some of the more common sales personas I have witnessed, but you may have seen or exhibited others. This is a good time to pause and ask yourself whether any of my example personas or any of the ones that flew through your mind while reading this chapter tend to be at the forefront of your sales processes, particularly when you are under stress. When you are relaxed and present, you likely pull approaches from a wide range of personas, leveraging what you think will work in a given situation. The key is that when you're relaxed, you have choice. If you are at the end of a quarter and a prospect has taken forever on minor contract revisions, it might be a good time to bring a bit more force to a conversation. In that case, you are intentionally using a tool versus being at the mercy of an out-of-control persona.

The persona game, like many other elements introduced in this part of the book, is just to build awareness of what is happening in you—both in your selling activity and in your life. The objective is to move from reactivity to awareness to choice. Those moves will radically increase your sales effectiveness.

Take a moment and consider a persona or two that reliably surfaces in your life, at work, or in selling contexts. Get creative and a bit playful and name those personas with memorable monikers.

Once you are armed with an understanding of an essence quality or two and some of your personality traits and personas, I recommend digging deeper into the facets of your unique personality style.

PERSONALITY TYPING TOOLS AND THE ENNEAGRAM

You can tell by now that I am a big believer in growing self-understanding to optimize your business-building prowess. It therefore ought to come as no surprise that I value personality typing systems to increase awareness of core personality patterns. I use personality typing as an added tool to improve my understanding of my motivations and increase my empathy with clients, business partners, friends, and family. I encourage you to do the same.

There are a host of valuable personality typing systems used to great advantage in business, including the Myers-Briggs Type Indicator (MBTI), the DISC assessment, StrengthsFinder, and the Birkman Method. The personality system I value most to increase my and my clients' understanding of core personality patterns at the motivational level is the Enneagram.

The Enneagram categorizes personalities in nine types based primarily on motivation. The system answers the question of why different people (or types) do what they do. The figure offers a basic summary of the nine types.

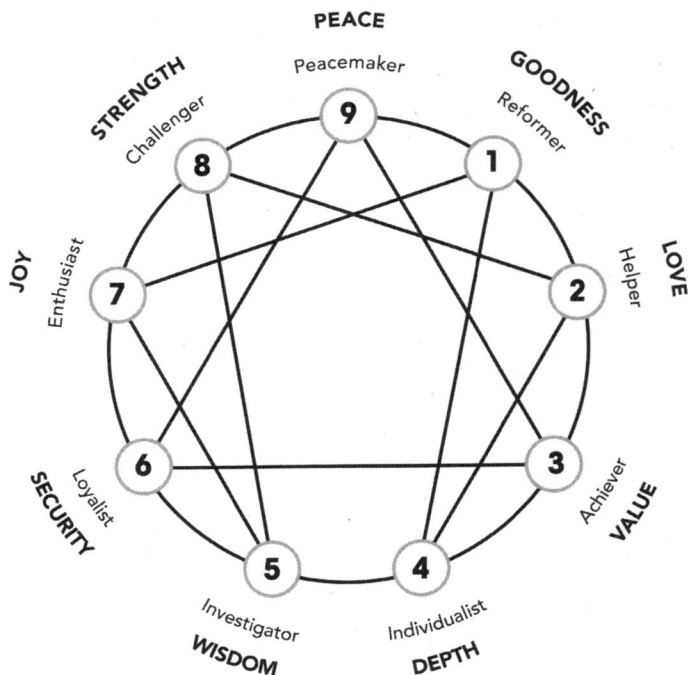

Everyone has a primary Enneagram type. That's the one that sheds the most light on a person's core patterns, particularly when they are feeling stressed, triggered, or caught in reactivity. Although you have only one "home" Enneagram type, most people have other types that also influence their thinking and approaches. These are often adjacent to the home type. In addition, most people can draw on the "best" qualities of every type when they are in an open, curious, nontriggered state.

Each type has a shorthand name, shown in capital letters in the figure. Each type also is associated with one essence quality that represents that type at its best: open, curious, and expansive. The essence quality offers a motivational through line for that type. The essence quality for each type is listed underneath the type name in the graphic. You can think of this as the easiest path to understanding a person of that type. When you see a person through the lens of their type, you can appreciate that the reliable, lovable essence quality is in either the foreground or the background. For instance, a Type 9 Peacemaker prefers situations where the waters are calm, people get along, and conflict is minimal. A Type 3 Achiever prefers to contribute value, accomplish the unexpected, and win.

That said, each type also carries with it a "shadow side," or an "Achilles' heel," which is most often correlated with the essence quality. For a Type 3, winning can become winning at all costs or winning at the expense of authenticity or connection. For a Type 9, peacemaking can come at the cost of avoiding conflict and zoning out. When each type is under stress or in a triggered state, it reverts to those shadow qualities, which are often recognizable to the person of that type (through a lifetime of feedback) and to friends, partners, and coworkers of that person (who often give the feedback). Because the Enneagram is a personality system, I encourage people endeavoring to type themselves to consider which shadow (less lovely) qualities of a given type sound most like them when they are not at their best.

I use the Enneagram with clients and teams to understand their context and motivations of their behavior toward others in their best and less optimal moments. Remember, in nontriggered moments, our essence qualities shine. In triggered moments, when we feel under threat, resistant, or defensive, our personality traits come to the fore. I love the Enneagram system because it is, in my view, accessible at an elementary level and has layers of specialization to meet the learning desires of an avid practitioner.

TYPE	TYPE NAME	ESSENCE QUALITY	TRIGGERED STATE
1	Reformer	Goodness	Resentment, perfectionism, righteousness
2	Helper	Love	Pride, wanting to be seen as the helpful one, prioritizing others' needs above their own
3	Achiever	Value	Deception, seeking external validation, manipulating people and situations to be seen as successful, achievement treadmill
4	Individualist	Depth	Envy, wanting to be seen as unique and special, emotional sensitivity becomes oversensitivity
5	Investigator	Wisdom	Avarice, hoarding time for deep inquiry and problem-solving, unable to make decisions for lack of perfect information
6	Loyalist	Security	Anxiety, turning the gift of seeing risk into uncalibrated risk avoidance, slow to trust
7	Enthusiast	Joy	Gluttony, pursuing all the shiny objects, failing to meet agreements, flighty
8	Challenger	Strength	Lust, making every matter urgent and intense, using force to bully others and win
9	Peacemaker	Peace	Sloth, opting out of difficult moments to avoid conflict, taking the easy path and making the path easy for all

When I am selling my executive coaching and facilitation work, I often mention to prospects my Enneagram personality type. I do this because if a prospect is acquainted with the system, my type gives them an understanding of tendencies that might arise in my coaching. You may choose to learn your Enneagram type and use it as one means of sharing your tendencies in whatever you-focused work you are selling.

I'm a Type 8, nicknamed the challenger.

Since I'm all too familiar with the best and less lovable features of a Type 8, I often choose to share my best qualities and blind spots as a coach using this lens. For example, as a Type 8, I am extremely direct. At my best, this is a superpower. I share my opinions about what I am hearing or seeing without a filter. At my best, I remember that just because I have an opinion doesn't make me right. Like any great quality, my directness can go sideways. If I am triggered, threatened, or having a rough day, unattached directness can start to look like petulance and even anger. I'm rarely in the latter states when I am working; however, if I'm in a prospect conversation with someone who wants to work with someone more soothing, confirming, and supportive, I'm not their person. No problem. Most of the people who hire me to coach, consult, or facilitate are looking for someone who tells it like it is.

As you engage in your own personal deep dive to build your enhanced vision of you for sales and your business, I recommend that you use a respected personality evaluation tool to give you this added layer of understanding. You can type yourself using the Enneagram or your tool of choice.

Because I'm so focused on the Enneagram, and because I will invite you to take the test as an exercise at the end of this chapter, I'd like to share a few strengths and potential challenges for each Enneagram type in selling.

TYPE	SALES STRENGTH	SALES CHALLENGE
1—Reformer	Excels at sales operations and processes like Salesforce compliance	Gets rigid during negotiations around engagement terms
2—Helper	Builds strong relationships with prospects	Concedes meaningful deal points to accommodate prospects' objections
3—Achiever	Generates big prospect funnels and closes quickly and effectively at desirable prices and terms	Oversells and glosses over details Contorts to be whatever a prospect needs to get to a yes on a sale
4—Individualist	Finds creative, unconventional ways to develop lucrative business relationships	Becomes self-critical when a deal isn't the most vision- and values-aligned for her or her company
5—Investigator	Develops data-driven sales approaches that pave the way to objective, obvious closes	Struggles to build strong connections through the deal cycle due to focus on data and processes
6—Loyalist	Creates realistic expectations for a future business relationship that instill confidence	Gets anxious about whether the project plan can really work Fails to paint a big enough vision of what's possible due to anxiety
7—Enthusiast	Casts a wide net of prospects for a new product or service and attracts the interest of highly desirable customers	Fails to follow through on the basic, operational elements of the sales process
8—Challenger	Makes inroads to the most powerful people and prospects without fear	Makes compromises on deal terms difficult due to taking adamant positions on issues
9—Peacemaker	Instills confidence in prospects due to authenticity and low-pressure tactics	Faces challenges in getting to a close at strong terms due to unwillingness to engage in conflict

EXERCISE

Get to Know Your Essence Qualities and Sales Personas

- Name two of your essence qualities. You might have done this earlier in this chapter.
- Name two personality traits or personas that you sometimes (consciously or unconsciously) bring to the fore in an uncomfortable situation. For many, thinking about a cocktail party, a wedding where you know only the bride, a networking event, or a family gathering might be a good start.
- Next, identify one of your sales-related personas. I mentioned a few sales personas in this chapter. Find one of yours, which may show up as a strong belief you hold or a reliable behavior you engage in during the sales process. Give that persona a memorable name to get to know it better. Naming personas makes the process of learning about your personality parts or personas more playful in moments when it might otherwise be self-punishing.
- Once you've identified one of your sales-related personas, interview that persona. Stay with me here. I mean that you will be "interviewing" a trait or persona that is part of you for your own benefit. You want to gain a sense of the motivations, benefits, and costs of these personas. To do that, ask them the following:
  - » What's one thing you want for [your name]?
  - » What's one thing you're scared of?
  - » What's one way you make [your name]'s life better?
  - » What's one thing you cost [your name]?
  - » If [your name] is going into a conversation, what would allow you to let them handle that conversation on their own?

This interview of your sales persona is intended to raise your awareness of less conscious behaviors that may arise during a sales conversation. Once you increase your understanding of these traits, you have a far better chance of channeling, leveraging, or minimizing their impact at any given moment in the sales process.

============= **EXERCISE** =============

Learn Your Enneagram Personality Type

A great business builder can be any personality type, but to be phenomenal, it's wise to increase your awareness of your internal operating system so you have a better sense of how to deploy your strengths and address your weaknesses in the context of growing your business. Discovering your type will help you do this.

- Take the Enneagram personality test. I recommend the Full RHETI test at www.enneagraminstitute.com. You'll find other free versions online, but I suggest this paid, more comprehensive version. The cost at the time of publication is $20 for a single test.
- Once you take the assessment and identify your Enneagram personality type, consider how that type can be helpful in your sales efforts and how certain positive or less positive aspects of your type might undercut you in growing your business. Use the charts in this chapter to give you added insights.
- If your Enneagram personality type strengths and weaknesses resonate with you, you have the option to take steps (awareness at a minimum) to lean into strengths and address challenges.

CHAPTER 11

YOUR ZONE OF GENIUS

You're developing a fuller understanding of who you are. This is the you that you will be selling. As the next step in deepening your awareness, I recommend developing an appreciation of what you are doing or how you are being in your zone of genius. You are more likely to be successful in selling a business that is focused on you if your business makes you feel happy, enlivened, extraordinary, and in flow. That's genius. Before you can intentionally lean in, you want to understand your personal genius landscape.

The concept of a zone of genius comes from Gay Hendricks's book *The Big Leap: Conquer Your Hidden Fear and Take Life to the Next Level*. Hendricks identifies the four zones of capability as the zone of incompetence, zone of competence, zone of excellence, and zone of genius.

YOUR ZONE OF INCOMPETENCE

This, not surprisingly, represents things you are not very good at. For me, one clear example is residential plumbing and electrical. If I invite you to a home for which I've installed the electrical system, bring a candle. Most high-performing people in the midst of running an established one-person services business are not often in their zone of incompetence. They're surely not selling services in that zone. However, in any early-stage company or, for that matter, any company that is having a really bad day, we may often find ourselves doing work that lives in our zone of incompetence.

When I set up my first e-commerce business, this happened daily. I was learning so much every day, and my modest revenue made it seem unwise to hire an expert in the many things at which I was wholly incompetent— website development, manufacturing efficiencies, shipping processes, Photoshop. So I learned by necessity. That was fine. Today, running my executive coaching business, I have a team that supports me in my areas of incompetence. I'm lousy at handling bureaucracy on the phone, and in fact, I rarely answer my phone. I have a hard time managing details of in-person events when I have a week that includes meetings, hosted dinners, and the like. I still am not great at web development. So I have people who do these things better than I do, allowing me to minimize the amount of time I spend in my zone of incompetence.

YOUR ZONE OF COMPETENCE

This encompasses those tasks you are okay at. You are good enough to get the job done, perhaps even done well, but it is more of a slog, you don't exceed expectations, and you acutely feel how much better others would be at that task. This is a far more common place for new founders, companies, solopreneurs, and cash-strapped nonprofits to spend their time. It might also be a zone you're in at home if you're saving money for a major purchase or paying down student loans. A zone of competence for me is deep cleaning my bathroom. I was a hotel housekeeper in college for a time, so I'm not half bad at this. I understand the steps needed to quickly make a bathroom grime- and hair-free. On the business side, I am decent at building visually and verbally compelling slides for presentations. In my early career and at early-stage companies, I often played in this zone. Without a lot of organizational layers, this is part of any entrepreneurial venture, including, perhaps, your business focused on selling you.

YOUR ZONE OF EXCELLENCE

The more complex area, your zone of excellence, comprises things you do (or ways that you are) in which you truly excel. If you're working for a larger company that has had a greater opportunity to get the right people in the right seats, you're likely getting plenty of opportunities to be excellent. If you've started working in a you-centric company, and you have a few committed paying customers, you're doubtless operating often in your zone of excellence as well. When I started my solopreneur company, my first offerings were squarely in my zone of excellence. My 2013 website shows that I marketed these four things:

+ Branding and digital marketing
+ Sales and business development
+ Strategic planning
+ Executive and team activation

Most of these services were things I had been doing for many years as a founder and leader in tech startups. I was afraid to even mention coaching! This made sense. I was good at these things. People knew me to be good at them. I could talk about these things and credibly pitch clients on them.

When you're in your zone of excellence, you get plenty of validation. You earn promotions and awards. You are recruited to bigger and "better" roles. Your parents gush about you when you're not around. This is why most successful professionals top out in their zone of excellence. The praise is reassuring; you've mastered these areas. Staying in that zone is positive and comfortable.

Like all you superb humans, I have a wealth of things in my zone of excellence. I excel at writing marketing pitches, naming companies, conducting a "vision, mission, values" workshop, and bringing an executive team together to refine and become aligned around a strategic plan. Those are all solidly in the zone of excellence for me.

When I began my solopreneur company, I stayed close to the dock, offering these kinds of close-to-the-business services. Things went great. But I started to notice that I wasn't as energized about these tasks: the prep work, the post work, the outcome-driven engagement style. Then I started to notice that even when I was doing a vision, mission, and values workshop, I was actually doing an executive coaching engagement with a little content spread around it. I started to see, furthermore, that I was bringing many of my coaching contexts and tools to dinner parties and chats with friends, enlivening those discussions even more. It was the coaching- and context-driven facilitation—not the content—that was most invigorating to me. That feeling of aliveness offers a hint that you're seeing past your zone of excellence to an even more interesting—and often seemingly risky—place. It is a sure signal of the zone of genius.

YOUR ZONE OF GENIUS

Just when you're successful and comfortable, you get a chance to wonder about the next area of your personal growth and development. Sorting this out in the early stages of selling a solopreneur business (and reevaluating this often) is a great tool for your personal satisfaction and for your success. There is nothing better than working with someone who is working in their zone of genius. And there is nothing easier to sell than you when you're selling your zone of genius.

When you're in your zone of genius, not only are you excellent at doing the thing you are doing (or being the way you are being), but doing the thing feels effortless. Time falls away. You're in flow. Being in one's zone of genius offers access to one's full potential and maximum creativity.

For me, serving as the mistress of ceremonies for awards shows is in my zone of genius. It's public speaking, and I was adept at that shortly before I started walking. I love the chance to engage an audience; I love celebrating the award recipients; I love the real-time opportunities to be funny and dynamic (core value alert!) in reaction to things that happen in the events; and I love surprising the awardees with fun facts I've learned about them in my deep research.

Want to know another thing that is certainly in my zone of genius? Selling! Even talking about selling. That's why, after a decade of thinking about books I could write and doing some writing on my blog about topics such as coaching, leadership, and investing in women-led companies, I finally wrote this book. As I started writing, I noticed the magnetic pull to writing more and writing quickly. The words came through me. I felt a little fear, but I quickly realized that writing this book about a topic squarely in my zone of genius didn't feel like work. It felt like an exercise of pure joy and expansive creativity. It didn't hurt that I'd read Anne Lamott's *Bird by Bird*. Was my first draft lousy? Yes. Yes, it was. But even my lousy draft was marked by the insights, conviction, and electricity of someone operating in their zone of genius.

BARRIERS TO THE ZONE OF GENIUS

As I mentioned, there are many reasons why we consciously or unconsciously choose to not live in our zone of genius. We may believe that it's not possible. We may feel that it's risky to give up a reliable and rewarding job in our zone of excellence. We may believe that it's financially irresponsible to lean into our zone of genius—which is why it's important to understand your upper limits and unconscious commitments.

Moreover, I have heard from clients that the idea of a zone of genius can create some self-defeating thinking. That spin might go like this: "I heard about this genius thing, and I'm sure I'm not in that because I do get tired, I do notice time, and I don't think I'm a genius very often. I'm feeling a lot of unhelpful pressure to find my zone of genius and live in it!" If you read about this concept and have that storyline running through your mind, I would encourage you to take one lesson from this concept: The idea of a zone of genius is most useful as a vehicle to allow you to see when you might be "settling for" being in your zone of excellence as the peak state of your potential.

The awareness of genius makes it simpler to recognize your zone of excellence. You ought to be in excellence often, because you read this far under the presumption that you are superb at something. Consider those moments in excellence when you feel most drained and simply remember that there may be a different path—this path called genius. There's nothing to do right now. No pressure. No judgment. Just build your awareness of when you are in your zone of excellence and how that may not be the highest and greatest use of your gifts in the world. The rest—spotting opportunities for what else might be possible—will likely unfold from your self-awareness.

For now, however, let's inquire about what your zone of genius may be. My theory is that the more you are selling work that happens in your zone of genius, the more successful you will be in selling that work.

EXERCISE
The Best Stuff

This exercise, based on the work of Jim Warner and Kaley Klemp, will help you find your zone of genius. It encourages you to identify common threads across memorable accomplishments or experiences in your life. These threads point to your unique gifts. Here's how you do it:

- Jot down four to eight "stories" or snapshots from your life of moments when you were at your best. These may be moments of accomplishment or peak experiences. They are moments when you enjoyed what you were doing and believed that you did that thing well.
- Your stories can be from work or from leisure activities, hobbies, travel, or relationships.
- Focus on what has been meaningful to you rather than what others may have deemed important or valuable.
- Include what you actually did, what talents or skills you used, and what felt meaningful in the experience.
- Make your snapshot stories no more than one or two sentences.

Once you have your stories, bring them to your personal board of directors meeting, or just speak to a few friends. Read them your stories and ask them to jot down common themes across aspects of your stories. Examples might include "You enjoy boiling down complexity to simple insights," "You relish time with intimates when you are simply 'being' rather than 'doing,'" "You prefer strategic thinking to regular task completion," "You work harder when your accomplishments are public," or "You enjoy underpromising and overdelivering." As you garner input from a group of close friends or coworkers, keep your own distilled list of the themes that resonate with you.

Once you have a few zone of genius themes, consider leaning into those themes in the work you are doing, the engagements you are choosing, the materials you use to talk about your solopreneur business, and your sales pitches.

Armed with your two-minute bio, your top two core values, and your zone of genius themes, you are ready to dial in the focus of a business that centers on you. Even better, you are ready to pitch that business from a place of authenticity, aliveness, and flow. The goal is not to live and work in your zone of genius 100 percent of the time. But if you are taking the risk and the trouble to form your own company that depends on your gifts, setting a goal of designing that business around being in your zone of genius 50 percent of the time seems like a reasonable and aspirational target. I have a very talented executive business partner (an instrumental executive assistant who functions like a partner in many ways) who handles many tasks in my zones of incompetence, competence, and even excellence. Yet I still need to take out the trash, go to the dentist, renew my driver's license, and shop for groceries. Regarding my personal balance, I think I'm in my zone of genius about 70 percent of the time across every area of my life. That stuns and amazes me most days.

EXERCISE
Deeper Dive: Zones of Capability Inventory

Since I often coach executives in moments of transition, I crafted another way to get familiar with your zone of genius and your willingness to live in that zone. Whether you are already working in a you-focused business or you're embarking on one, this exercise will help you gain clarity about where your true commitment lies.

This exercise takes some work. I created it to help you see through the noise of habit, external validation, and comfort zones. When my clients ask me for help in a search for a new role or in finding more life in a current role, this is my new go-to move.

I like using a spreadsheet for this, and the figure shows the template that I use.

A	B	C	D
Everything I Do Now	**Refined List of What I Do**	**Examples of What I Do**	**Zone: G, E, C, I**
Every single thing you do in your job	*Merge similar tasks or roles*	*Three recent instances of you doing that thing*	*The zone in which that thing lives*

The "board" feature in Asana, Trello, or Airtable will work, too. See the figure for an example of the board structure.

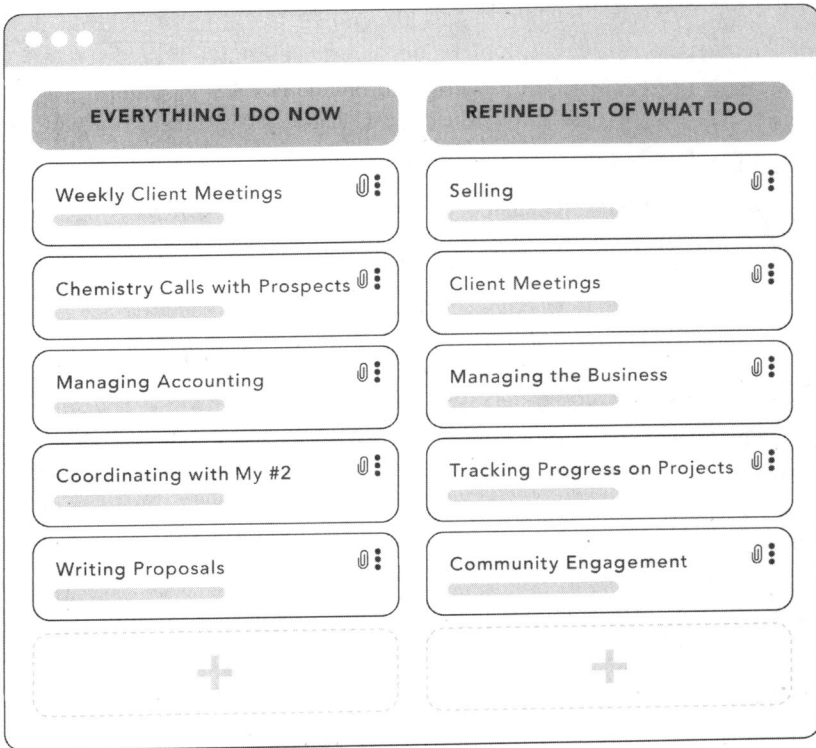

EVERYTHING I DO NOW	REFINED LIST OF WHAT I DO
Weekly Client Meetings	Selling
Chemistry Calls with Prospects	Client Meetings
Managing Accounting	Managing the Business
Coordinating with My #2	Tracking Progress on Projects
Writing Proposals	Community Engagement

First, create Column 1: Everything I Do Now. Write down every single thing you do in your job. Make this an exhaustive data dump with one task or focus area per row. For example, include different things you do to manage up: attending all-hands meetings, relating with other leaders, and ensuring that the boss's favorite coffee is in the cabinet. Don't worry about overlap or whether an entry is "important." Just open the floodgates here. This is an on-the-ground view of what you do.

Second, create Column 2: Refined List of What I Do. Refine Column 1 by blending similar specific tasks into a five-thousand-foot description of a slightly broader task. A good example is "managing up" or "handling financial tasks." Don't go to twenty thousand feet; we don't want to get too abstract. Make Column 2 a distilled list of things you do and roles you play.

Third, create Column 3: Examples of What I Do. In this column, write down three mini-moments or stories of you doing that thing recently where you've felt either a positive or a negative feeling. Limit these examples to the last two years. In a board, you might put the three examples inside Column 2 as a description, as I've done in the following example.

Fourth, read the little moments and stories you jotted down. Put yourself in the mindset of that thing you do. Feel the feeling of that activity in Column 2 in the context of your examples in Column 3. The goal here is to become very clear about real tasks you do and how you feel while doing them. Do this step with time and patience. This is a nice weekend activity.

Managing the Business

Assignee	
Due Date	

Projects *Refined List of What I Do* ⊗

Description
1. Coordinated tax matters with the accountant
2. Checked on time lag in receivables
3. Scheduled 1:1 meetings for new 360 project

Fifth, create Column 4: G (Genius), E (Excellence), C (Competence), or I (Incompetence) for each of the aforementioned zones. Having reviewed your item in Column 2 and the examples in Column 3, ask yourself, one row at a time, "In which zone does this item live? Is it my zone of incompetence, competence, excellence, or genius?" Use Column 4 to indicate the zone. If you are working in a board format, create a column for each zone and move tasks accordingly. See the figure for how this might look.

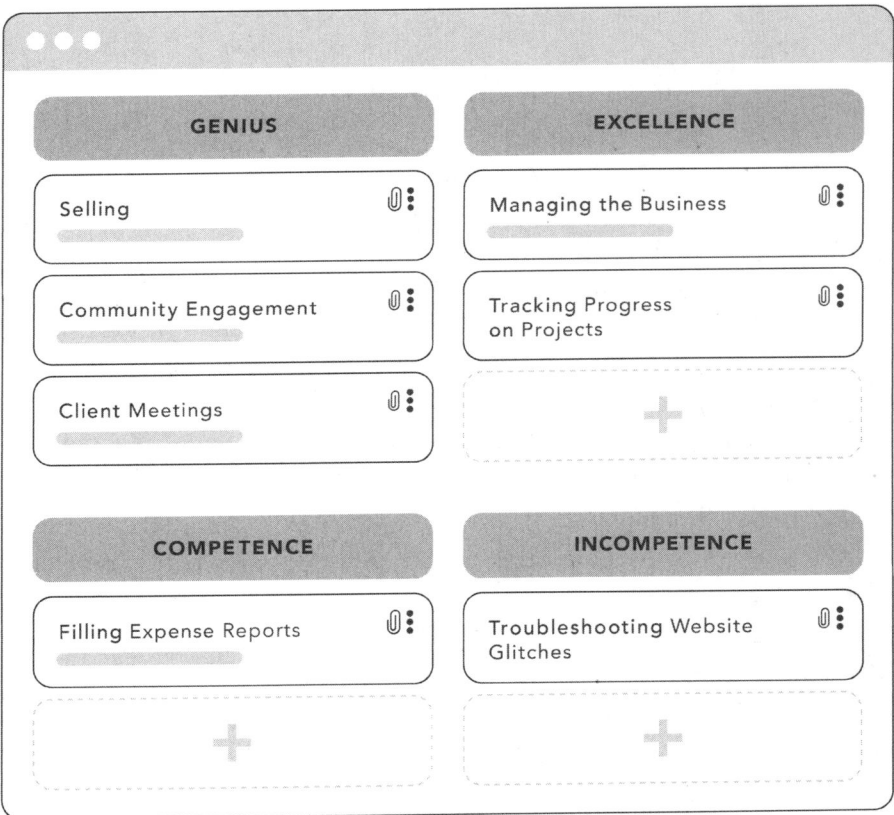

Sixth, look at your final four columns and ask yourself some questions:

+ What thoughts, stories, or conclusions arise as you reflect on the weight of things in different columns?

+ What do you notice about the distinction between tasks in your zone of excellence and those in your zone of genius?
+ How much are you doing in zones of competence and incompetence? What are the controlling stories for why that's occurring right now?
+ Do you want to lean into items in your zone of genius in your current or next role (or tomorrow in your current role)? Are you willing to?

===================== **EXERCISE** =====================

What to Let Go of to Spend More Time in Your Zone of Genius Today

Another reason we resist living more in our zone of genius is a sense of obligation, habit, or compromise. We say yes when we know that we would rather say no. We forget that every time we say yes but feel a no, we are saying no to something else to which we might feel a yes. And the latter thing just might stretch us to our zone of genius.

This exercise will give you a sense of where you may create a new boundary to give yourself permission to say no, freeing up space to say yes to choices that are more enlivening.

First, take a Post-it note, index card, or napkin. Draw a four-square court on it. (Two lines create four boxes. Red rubber ball and asphalt not required.)

Second, jot down your four primary areas of focus for the next month. Make these more general than "Take out the trash once a week" and more specific than "Solve climate change." Steer clear of grouped things like "Transform the marketing team by adding paid search, building out an Instagram channel, and creating a content marketing flywheel." Tie your focus areas to the current reality of your work and life on a one-month time horizon. These focus areas need not be measurable; they are simply four things to which you want to pay attention.

Stay with your gut. Avoid the magnetic attraction of obligation. Forget what people might think of you. Be sure you have a full-body yes to all four things. You're doing this exercise alone; be honest.

The figure shows mine (and yes, I had to shoo away some stories about selfishness to get to this).

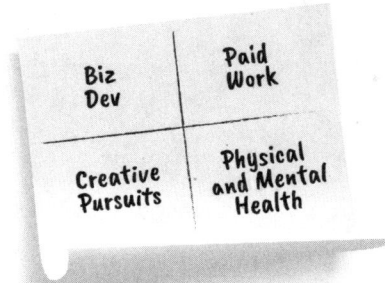

Third, look at your four boxes and be sure they're consistent with the aforementioned criteria. Then circle the one that, when you really check your authentic motivations, is truly the most important to you. See the figure for mine.

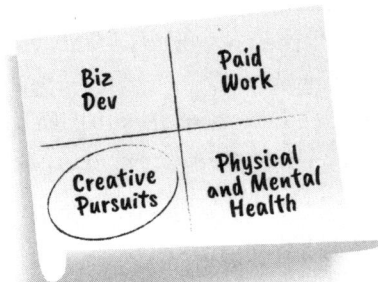

Fourth, turn over your Post-it and on the back, using the same level of abstraction and one-month time horizon, write down one thing you imagine you would need to let go of to truly focus on your top four. This is another place for honesty. The thing you might need to let go of is probably something that gives you material benefits (affirmation, validation, adrenaline, money, pride). It's important to remember that a commitment to honoring your yeses requires some willingness to let go of the noes and the maybes.

The figure shows mine, acknowledging both a want and a need to decline "pick your brain" meeting requests for the month.

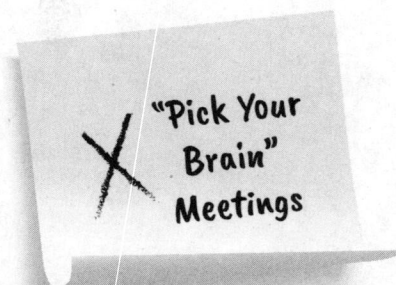

Fifth, if you want to go one step further, ask one person who loves you to do one simple task that might give you even more accountability around your areas of focus. Perhaps you need to face your aversion to letting other people down. If so, a nice accountability push might be to have your person email you on each of the next four Fridays to ask whom you let down that week (real or imagined). If the answer is no one, you likely missed a chance to lean into your zone of genius.

I want to acknowledge how hard it is to give up the thing you say you need (or want) to give up. There are unconscious commitments to that thing. That's why you've been doing it. So be gentle with yourself. This exercise is not designed for self-flagellation. It is an inquiry oriented toward building self-awareness and leaning into your zone of genius.

CHAPTER 12

NAMING YOUR GOALS

Any discussion of sales requires a consideration of goals or a definition of success. For the decade in which I've been running my coaching and facilitation business, my top three goal buckets in priority order have been revenue, calendar flexibility, and percentage of time in my zone of genius. Each of these goals is associated with my joy and freedom. When I have financial ease, time flexibility, and a flow state around my work, I am happier. Often exhilarated.

In Jerry Seinfeld's 2024 commencement speech at Duke University (coincidentally one of my alma maters), he spoke of the wonders of gratifying work:

> You know how they always say nobody ever looks back on their life and wishes they spent more time at the office? Well, why? Why don't they? Guess what? Depends on the job. If you took a stupid job that you find out you hate and you don't leave, that's your fault.
>
> Don't blame work. Work is wonderful. I definitely will not be looking back on my life wishing I worked less. If that's not how you feel at work, quit. On your lunch break. Disappear. Make people go, "What happened to that guy?" "I don't know, he said he was getting something to eat. Never came back."

If you are a solopreneur or a seller engaged in a business where growing revenue or delivering a service depends materially on you, I hope you're happy. As a reminder, I made multiple material career changes before I got to this "job" that is deeply gratifying.

MAPPING YOUR GOALS

Assuming your business goals are associated with living a satisfied life, as mine are, I've outlined a map of my business goals in hopes my analysis is of service to you in outlining yours.

Goal One

Increasing revenue. I have a constant eye on revenue. I use QuickBooks online for all my economics, from invoicing to profit-and-loss reports to expense tracking for taxes. I use Asana, my task management system, to forecast what I believe my revenue will look like throughout the year. If you ask me on any day, I know what my year-to-date revenue is, and I generally will have a ballpark figure for my accounts receivable. I don't track expenses at all. Why? Because net profit is not one of my goal buckets! If I were losing money, or close, I'm sure I'd pay more attention, but that's happily not an issue for me (and it almost surely won't be an issue for you if you're in a services business that depends primarily on you). My client-related travel expenses are reimbursed, and when I take business on referral, the 20 percent referral fee I pay to the referrer doesn't create any profitability risk.

From day one, I set an annual top-line revenue goal. In year one, my goal was to earn enough to equal the base compensation I had earned in the previous year as a tech executive. Every year since, I have had a goal of growing that number by a certain percentage. After a few years of dramatic growth, I realized I had unconsciously developed a BHAG, a term created by famed business writer Jim Collins in *Built to Last*. BHAG is pronounced "bee-hag" and is short for a "Big Hairy Audacious Goal." I highly recommend having a BHAG for some goal of yours. Mine was to hit $1 million in revenue in one calendar year. I did that in year six, and only a few people knew that before I decided to share it in this book. I am sharing it here because I am proud of it and because I want you to know that working on your own thing, if you're good and you do all the right things to be successful, can become very lucrative.

I revisit my goals at the end of every year. At the start of my ninth year, I decided to set a goal of reducing my revenue. The reason?

Goal Two

Scheduling flexibility. I realized in that BHAG year that I was working more than I wanted or needed to. I was achieving some of my financial goals on the top line (and in my retirement savings, funding of nieces' 529 accounts, and so on), and I wanted some time back. Because one of the key inputs for my coaching and consulting business is my time, I decided to force myself to earn less in service of having more free time.

You may think that sounds crazy. And you may be right. I have learned again and again that I can work less and still earn more. I'll talk more about this in the pricing chapter, but scarcity is a fantastic selling and pricing tool. What I was beginning to understand is that selling itself was so exciting for me that I was unconsciously compromising my scheduling flexibility in the heat of closing the next sale. I've shared that a zone of genius is selling. It's not easy to slow down on something that is so exhilarating. Moreover, in March, say, I was likely to be selling a gig I wouldn't do until August. My future self was developing some resentment for the lusty seller who had won earlier in the year.

My pivot to selling less business required a strict conversation with myself. It wasn't easy. It still is not easy. But it is paying dividends. I am hustling less, giving up fewer personal commitments with an excuse of "work," and referring more business to my partners. I will also talk more about referral networks later.

So much of our collective life has shifted with always-on tools, work from home, and far more porous boundaries between work and not-work, but I still experience the pure bliss of a partially or fully open calendar on a weekday. Do you know how nice it is to go on a popular hike on a weekday? Have you been to Costco on a Tuesday? Do you realize how much less time it takes to do almost anything when most people are working? Do you know how nice it is to do a yoga class at 9 a.m. on a Wednesday? Or to just go sit in the park on a blanket in the 10 a.m. sun? Holy moly, I do. It's beyond liberating.

So scheduling flexibility is one of my goal buckets. And I work on it. I still find myself compromising around scheduling flexibility. I can slip into a habit of setting a few hours of coaching time on many days instead of more hours on one day. I can make up a story that if I'm not "very available," I will lose business. I know that often the opposite is true—the less available I am, the more sought-after I am. You'll learn more about using scarcity of your availability as a tool later in the context of how that mindset can form a pillar of passionate ambivalence. You can't make up something like time scarcity as a fake reason to charge more, but you can set priorities in your life, and if you end up with less time for client work, your value as a resource and your revenue per hour might increase.

How do I maintain revenue and increase my scheduling flexibility?

Goal Three

Increase time in my zone of genius. With revenue strong, I have been highly focused on working with people and in situations that are squarely in my zone of genius. For me, it's a delicious obsession to become even more specific and aligned around what I'm doing and how I'm feeling when I'm at my best, to notice the exceptions, and to spot when I'm doing something that's a drain on my energy. The latter experience is proof that I've been in my zone of excellence. It's okay if I'm there or in my other zones at times—when I'm cooking, fixing a small broken thing in my home, folding laundry, or even fielding a time-sensitive request from a client to shape a message for an all-company communication—but at this point, there's no reason for me to be there at work anymore.

I want to point out that working in my zone of genius has tremendous value to my clients who are engaged with me in that zone. Often, in those engagements, we are both in our zones of genius. And that is fire.

Katie Breen and Her Zone of Genius

After graduating from the University of Maryland as the valedictorian of the business school, Katie Breen had an offer from a prestigious New York marketing agency. Katie landed and excelled in what became two successive jobs with agencies—representing global credit card, cosmetics, and electronics brands. She realized, however, that the work she had so eagerly anticipated was uninteresting and wholly unconnected to her passion for advancing women's health causes.

While continuing to work in marketing roles, she applied for public health positions—all of which would have come with material pay cuts. But she never got past the first résumé screen due to a lack of a master's degree or formal experience in the field. Katie decided to leave the workplace for two years and secure a master's in public health so she could have the impact she craved. This was a courageous choice because she had funded 100 percent of her undergraduate expenses through scholarships, loans, and working three years as a resident advisor. She was giving up a full-time salary, taking on graduate student loans, and again hustling for scholarships and part-time jobs to fund her advanced degree.

She went big, gaining admission to and graduating from the Harvard T.H. Chan School of Public Health. Her plan worked. She is now VP of quality and strategy for the Colorado Perinatal Care Quality Collaborative, which strives to improve maternal and infant health through clinical practice, community engagement, policy, and advocacy.

Katie has moved from being a highly skilled marketing upstart to a dedicated nonprofit leader. The core talents and skills she brought to those roles were similar. But the move from jobs that felt empty to a career that felt purposeful was a true shift toward her zone of genius. Her work now increases access to reproductive care for women across her state. She is navigating large bureaucracies and solving funding gaps to make real change. Her intrinsic motivation is clear.

YOUR DEFINITION OF SUCCESS

I want you to decide right now what your definition of success is for your business on a one-, three-, and ten-year horizon. I want you to set checkpoints at which you will look at your goals and determine how you're performing against them. If the answer is "great," super. You can keep your goals where they are or reforecast to goals that seem more ambitious. And if, for some reason, you are not hitting your goals, I want you to use those same checkpoints to get curious. Were you off in your definition of success? Misaligned with your zone of genius and what you're offering? Not hitting the mark on selling?

Armed with your goals and your commitment to checking in with yourself (and people you love) in the future, you increase your chances of success and satisfaction.

There are different ways to think about goals for a solopreneur business. Here are the categories of goals I recommend considering:

+ Revenue
+ Net profit
+ Increase in earnings per unit of time (e.g., revenue per hour)
+ Overall growth rate, month over month or year over year
+ Scale or reach of your business
+ Ability to cover expenses or fund other big goals (buying a home, kids' education accounts, charitable contributions of money or time, etc.)
+ Your day-to-day satisfaction
+ Pride in your work
+ Reputation enhancement
+ Percentage of time in your zone of genius
+ Impact on an issue that matters to you, including the lives of others
+ Quality of relationships tied to work
+ Quantity of time spent not working or flexibility in scheduling your time

Some of these may resonate with you, and others may arise as you consider this list. In any event, I recommend that you narrow your focus to three top goals, and I recommend that you be highly specific. Also, I suggest that you revisit your goals at least once a year. If you're doing great, they will shift, and staying present with your objectives will increase your motivation, your sense of accomplishment, or your self-reflection about what might need to shift to get more of those first two things.

EXERCISE
Goal Buckets for You and One BHAG

From the aforementioned list or from other goal buckets that resonate for you, choose and force-rank your top three goal buckets.

Set three goals for each goal bucket: one year, two years, and BHAG.

EXERCISE
Five-Year Vision Statement

Imagine yourself in five years after incorporating the work you're doing in this book and the learning you're acquiring into your business or your career. Consider your personal life and what feels joyful and possible there. Then write a present-tense statement in a paragraph or two of what your life is like five years hence. Your goal buckets may be involved.

If you are wondering how this might look and sound, I asked my executive business partner, Liz Nelson, to share her statement:

> I make three times what I did when I started six years ago. Half of my revenue comes from steady client relationships, and half is from conducting 360 reviews of leaders. I have a website that is uniquely me and brings me one strong lead each month. I have expanded my service offerings to include workshops and small-group facilitation, so I have opportunities to teach again.
>
> My work schedule continues to be flexible to accommodate time for family fun and travel. I spend at least 75 percent of my time in my zone of genius or zone of excellence, and I occasionally turn down opportunities that are a bad fit. I work with people who value my time and expertise and who are up to good things in this world.

EXERCISE
What You Need to Let Go Of

Reflect on your one- and two-year goals and your five-year vision. What might you want or need to let go of to increase your odds of reaching those goals or your five-year vision? As an example, here's Liz:

> Mentally, I need to release my scarcity mindset and the related belief that I won't ever have (or deserve) abundance. More pragmatically, I will need to let go of saying yes without first vetting the ask or opportunity.

> Your turn.

PART 4

LAYING THE GROUNDWORK FOR SELLING

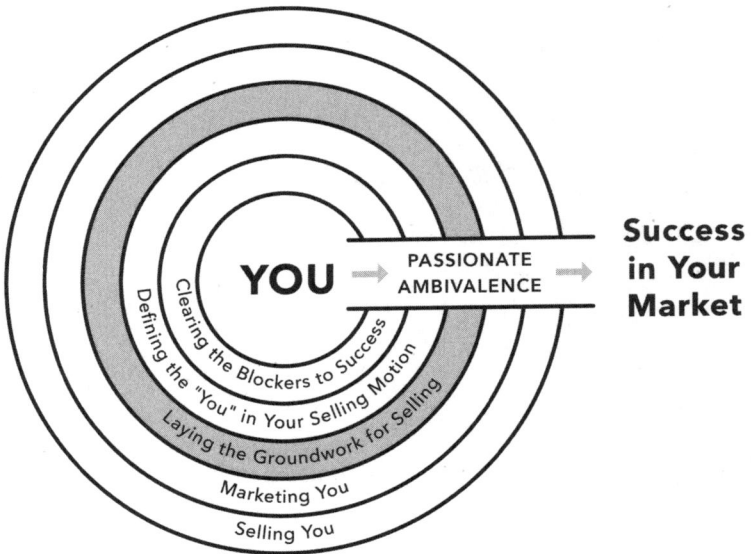

CHAPTER 13

HOW I STARTED
MY SOLOPRENEUR BUSINESS

As I mentioned, in my last official company job, I went from being chief growth officer at an established tech startup to unemployed in the span of twenty-four hours. In the few weeks that followed, I did everything I've suggested you do in the preceding chapters. During that lightning-fast build phase and for the ten years since, I have been avidly selling in the way I do. I have built this sales philosophy and these tactics over a near lifetime.

Not everything worked the first time. I will share some details about the early days of my company for two reasons. First, I have watched hundreds of new companies get off the ground, so the steps I took were not random but influenced by a meaningful pool of data about what works and what doesn't at the beginning. Second, the steps I will outline here are accessible for most people. They are basic and fundamental building blocks of the initial start for a business or sales effort focused primarily on you. As you read about the steps I've elected to focus on, consider what is and isn't relevant to your goals and stage.

You'll see that it took me a year or so of scrapping to get to the sales motion I use now. As a reminder, the trajectory I'm describing may not work for you if you are not superb. But if you've read this far, you surely must be (not because you know how to read but because you've kept reading through my repeated admonitions).

I started at zero revenue, as most of you will. Perhaps you have a leg up and the company you're leaving wants to be your first client for your new independent business. Brava. That's fantastic. I didn't have that, but dependence on a single client is still too risky. You will want to get scrappy to diversify your client base in any event.

This is how it happened for me, offered in service to you.

MY FIRST SITE

I launched a very slim website. That first site used "we" far more than "I" in describing my company. I've never shied away from looking bigger than I am. The service offerings were broad enough for people to think of me in a wide range of contexts. I was eager to see what might work. My "What we do" included the following:

- Branding and digital marketing
- Sales and business development
- Product development insight and ideation
- Leadership and team activation

This lineup of work buckets made sense at the time. I stayed *very close* to the things I knew I could do because I'd spent the previous years doing them as an executive at startup tech companies. I'm glad I did it this way, as it provided an on-ramp for quick wins and helped me clarify what I ultimately elected to focus on later. My first solo work fell into these operational categories. In hindsight, I can see that I smuggled my coaching and facilitation in through what seemed to me more marketable or at least obviously essential service categories. When I ran a half-day session on sales, for example, I would frequently introduce concepts like unconscious commitments when I felt that such a concept would be as helpful as or more helpful than a more on-the-nose sales topic.

If you are launching your first site, or marketing materials, or outreach email to a possible client, you also may consider being a bit broader about what you do than the very thing you want to do most. This is especially true if you don't know at the start exactly what you want to do most. This book offers a raft of exercises to help you gain clarity, but if acquiring that first client is important, try for breadth at the beginning. You always have the option of narrowing, and doing so is far easier with a roof over your head and fresh vegetables in the fridge (to add to the ramen in the pantry).

ANNOUNCING THAT I WAS OPEN FOR BUSINESS

After a very simple version of my site went live, I posted on every social media channel I used that my business was open and looking for clients that could benefit from the energy, smarts, and services I was offering. I got my first client from a Facebook friend who referred her husband to me. The focus of that engagement? Branding, marketing, and sales. With this first engagement and zero revenue to date, I decided to ask for a retainer. I got it! One thousand dollars a month. Average hourly rate: about $50. Did I celebrate that win? Yes. Yes, I did.

I reached out personally to hundreds of people in my network. I let local CEOs, venture capitalists, angel investors, professors, startup founders, former colleagues, and friends know that this was my new way of working. I asked them for introductions. The next year, and for the next decade, this worked. It was not a fire hose, but once every month or two, I received a note asking if I could do X for Y. My answer was almost always yes during the early years. A prominent venture capitalist had a client that needed a vision, mission, values workshop. Could I do that? Yes. Did I need to do some groundwork to create a program that would satisfy this need before walking in for a full-day workshop on these topics? Of course I did.

To launch your business, you will want to look across your network at every person you know who might be connected to a prospective client. This takes an enormous amount of work, but once you have your list—comprising in-person friends, influential social media contacts, your parents' friends, and the teachers and previous employers you're still in touch with who might help—you will be glad to have this cumulative and evolving list as a resource. It's worth noting that it's a resource to be closely guarded, carefully used, and never abused.

RUNNING MINI-MARKETING EXPERIMENTS

I also started running a series of experiments to find other work I could market.

I was already an established mentor in my community, so I knew people and had a decent reputation (as far as I knew). That meant I had a meaningful influx of requests for free pick-my-brain meetings. I was fine doing those. A role model of mine, venture capitalist Brad Feld, had modeled "random meetings" in my community of Boulder, Colorado. I had benefited from random meetings when I moved to town, and I wanted to repay that community karma. But as a matter of time management and business focus, I needed to shift *some* of these free coffee meetings to paid meetings. That seemed simple enough. I started offering $95 coffee meetings. People could talk to me about anything they wanted and get theoretically helpful perspectives from a somewhat seasoned outsider without a dog in the fight. It worked. I did a handful of these. I got testimonials for my site from them. I got at least one more regular coaching client from them. I didn't jettison my free meetings, but I made them shorter, less frequent, and available mainly to close friends and allies who could at some point potentially refer future work. Without a steady paycheck, I wanted (er, needed) to put more attention on revenue.

One example of how I scaled my free meetings for greater efficiency and impact was one of my favorite endeavors: the Booth. I have long disdained the experience of following my calendar from meeting to meeting. I also hated going to coffee shops and meeting people in person because it doesn't scale well. The Booth allowed me to sit in one of my favorite spots: the ten-person booth at the Corner Bar in Boulder. I could sit there for two hours and invite anyone who wanted to connect on any topic. This meant I responded to email requests for coffee with an invitation to the Booth. You don't have to squint too hard to see the relationship of this strategy to my online dating approach. People could sign up for the Booth. I said yes to no more than twenty-five people for each event, and I guaranteed that each person would get no fewer (and likely no more) than ten minutes with me to talk about anything: startups, investments, marketing, sales, consciousness, relationships, pizza. My dear friend and colleague at the time, Hannah

Davis, handled the gaggle of people who were waiting. I met my quota of giving. I had a blast. I had cider. People met other people, so these happenings created more community and more learning across the group. And the Booth created *more business*. That wasn't the point, but I firmly believe that the more you do, the more you do.

My examples may not be right for you, but I want you to look at the key elements they exhibit—a focus on community, giving my time, creating value for groups of people where I could—and see what in your life you might try out as a marketing lever. You may be active in your church, you may be a coach for your kid's T-ball team, you may be an avid triathlete. These environments, in real life and on social media, all offer opportunities to reach groups of people with whom you share hobbies or values and tell them about what you're up to in a way that makes them interested in supporting you.

TRYING OUT A FEW DIFFERENT "PRODUCTS"

I am an experimenter by nature. I try lots of things, and I don't put eons into any of them at the start because I don't want to be too attached to any one thing in case that thing fails. As such, I tried many different offerings to build interest (and revenue). I encourage you to consider, even if you're entering a path that seems well-defined, that as an entrepreneur, being creative in finding innovative ways to capture revenue will serve you.

I wanted to create half-day and two-day programs around conscious leadership. I wanted these programs to be akin to the immersive sessions I'd participated in during my early exposure to conscious leadership, but I wanted them to feel like me, and I wanted to leverage my operating background. I marketed these programs as Leadership Camps.

I didn't want to do these camps alone, so I recruited my best friend and favorite creative collaborator, Leah Pearlman, to join me. She is a talented coach and facilitator, and she has a résumé that made her a credible match for the business-meets-consciousness vibe I was after. I handled sales (zone of genius). I also developed and taught the curriculum during the camps.

Leah was the most incredible "color guy" ever. When a question arose that I couldn't answer, she was a genius at adding value in impromptu responses. She also brought elements to our partnership that I liked—somatic awareness, deep emotional intelligence, a flair for play and movement, and a sizzling sense of humor. One unique thing about our collaboration was that we would *practice* what we were teaching in front of our paid audience. When we disagreed, we did so publicly and used our candor tools to address the disagreement. When we had a "persona party," she once played me and I played her, modeling self- and other-awareness in a way that couldn't be taught from the curriculum. That persona party remains one of my favorite Leadership Camp memories.

Early camps were priced at $500 per person for two days, with a $100 early-bird discount. Leah reminded me that I called almost every attendee personally to invite them to come. Our first camp had thirty-five attendees. We did many. The price rose to $1,999 for a two-and-a-half-day camp. I launched three-hour remote mini-camps—introductions to the basics of conscious leadership—which attracted individuals and small groups from companies at an easy entry price of $199.

I had a program. A brand. A web presence. Hundreds of people referring others and a network of people who were learning conscious leadership from me and practicing actively in my town. These camps became fantastic lead generation for me—both for 1:1 executive coaching work and for leadership team programs that emulated camp.

Leadership Camp also gave rise to Couples Camp and a program about generational family wealth.

Flywheel. Flywheel. Flywheel. Things were getting interesting.

Leah and I also ran our first six-month Conscious Leadership Forum. We told people close to us (including previous camp attendees) that this was a complete experiment and that we had no idea what would happen. We priced that forum at hundreds instead of thousands of dollars per person, and we delivered on expectations of both doing something cool (many people repeated the forum for years at annually increasing price points) and messing things up (there was that evening when we disclosed to everyone that we honestly had no idea whether we were doing anything of value, and we wanted to reveal our insecurity).

REFLECTIONS AND TAKEAWAYS

Takeaway 1

Disappointment, impatience, and failure are positive indicators, even if they suck in the moment. When I look back at the early years of my solopreneur business, it seems so logical and wise. I hope you have this experience, too, and I hope the lessons and tactics in this book are part of your linear path, with each event a logical outgrowth of something that came before. However, I want to acknowledge that for me, it didn't always feel that way. It often felt like nearly haphazard experimentation. I want to normalize that feeling for you so that you don't freak out if something flops or if things aren't moving as quickly as you'd like. It's fine. In fact, if you don't feel a level of uncertainty at times, you likely aren't experimenting enough, or you haven't set ambitious goals. Hard emotions are worth acknowledging, feeling, and then using for your advantage in the next actions you take.

Takeaway 2

Always be learning. There's a famous line from a less famous movie, *Glengarry Glen Ross*. The setting is a sales boiler room, and the repeated line is "Always be closing." Don't get me wrong—that would be great. If your business is selling frozen lemonade only on 100-degree days in Phoenix, you'll likely nail it. If it is not, I would focus on always learning. If you're doing as much trial and error as I propose, you will have days, weeks, and an occasional month where nothing closes. That is fine if you are learning something from every flop or quiet period that will help you sell better, be better at what you do, or pivot to bring your business closer to alignment with your greatest strengths. As I look back on the early chapter of my independent business, there is not much I would advise my younger self (or you) to change. I learned foundational lessons, including how to turn my time into money; how to balance mentor and community time with paid work; how and when to convert mentor relationships to paid relationships (something I did with extreme caution and tons of authentic conversation); how to sneak my deepest passions into engagements that were not as interesting to me; how to create new monetization efforts around content I loved; how to build brands; how to partner with people who complemented my strengths; and how to build a reputation of trust that would ultimately generate the high-value, high-flexibility business I have now. If you are learning, great. If you are keeping a record of what you're learning for those low days when you might have forgotten what you learned, even better.

Takeaway 3

Keep dialing things in to discover what you most love to do. I have invited you several times to look for the intersection of what you love and what you're good at. If your efforts are jelling, you can get more and more specific about this over time. The more dialed in you are on what you love, the more you will attract your most desired customers on your most favorable business terms.

Your version of your early chapter (or the chapter you're in right now) will be your own. I offer mine to show the strengths and the compromises that were formative in my journey in case my story informs your outlook and plans.

EXERCISE
Next Meaningful Experiments at Your Stage

- If you think about your current situation—either just getting started or well into your efforts—what are three meaningful actions you could test starting next week?
- For each action, what three tactics will happen and in what order?
- For each tactic, how will you measure success? On what timeline will you decide to continue with that tactic or pivot to something else?

CHAPTER 14

SIX RELIABLE PRINCIPLES OF GETTING STARTED

T he following six principles helped me at the start and have remained consistent over time: fluid pricing, experimentation, improving my brand and research by association, partnership when it seems either accretive or fun, prioritizing my time through extreme discernment, and a process I call Pivot. Learn. Execute. Repeat.

FLUID PRICING

If you are early in a business or a selling process, it's quite likely that you don't know what the market will pay. You may know what you want, but early on, especially if you need to meet financial obligations, I recommend keeping an open mind on pricing. I have routinely watched startups become very large companies by using fluid pricing early and often. As they have scaled up their businesses, proven the value, found their customers, learned their true costs, and compared results to their financial goals, they have repriced and repackaged offerings on an ongoing basis.

I started working for very little money compared to what I charge today. My day rate today is twelve times what it was ten years ago. My pricing was fluid. I considered what I thought was fair and doable for someone look-ing to work with me. When 1:1 coaching was too pricey for three different people, I coached those three together as a coaching "pod." I made things work.

Starting in my second year, I had a floor for my pricing, which I would violate only if I wanted to engage in a pro bono endeavor for something I cared about. In those situations, I would generally work for free. So I have always earned at least my floor rate, or I have worked for free. My floor has simply increased radically over time.

EXPERIMENTATION AND FEEDBACK

I've discussed experimentation in many contexts. The bible for entrepre-neurship, *The Lean Startup* by Eric Ries, makes experimentation a key element in the build-measure-learn cycle for new companies. The entrepre-neurial mindset—often called a growth mindset—itself requires a blend of flexibility and agility to respond to uncertainty and changing circumstances. Experimentation and a nimble reaction to feedback are at the heart of that context.

I tried so many things at the start, and when I tried them, I would post them on my site and every social site as if they were happening. They were *definitely not happening* unless enough people signed up to make the program viable. But I was the only one who knew that. I presented these things as if they were mostly baked opportunities that were available to a select few people if they acted quickly. I didn't put them out in the world as trial bal-loons, even though they often were (and still often are). Many of these efforts would probably be considered failures. I simply pulled those attempts down from my site and kept trying other new things.

This isn't a perfect system. People often do sign up for these scheduled events and are disappointed when I cancel. I generally offer an alternative, something free, to offset this disappointment. I also transparently explain to them my process of selling, which sometimes leads to this result. Finally, I make these decisions quickly, so those who are interested have enough advance notice to change plans.

Pana's Experimentation to Find Its Business Model

Devon Tivona and Sam Felsenthal founded Pana as a "travel concierge" service for individual travelers. It was a remarkable user experience designed as a contemporary, digitally enabled, always-on travel agent. A traveler who subscribed to Pana in the early years paid a monthly fee and could book travel, change travel, and address travel hiccups on the app's very slick chat interface.

Devon and Sam tried everything to drive consumer demand for the app subscriptions, including selling "seat" licenses to companies that wanted to give their frequently traveling employees a tool to make travel easier. From the outside (and from my view as a customer and an investor myself), it seemed to be working. However, the Pana team started seeing that the business was difficult to manage with individual customers who were especially demanding. Complaints mounted. Customer service representatives were hired, and the app couldn't operate profitably for the users who were the most demanding. This was clear evidence for the founders of what startups call a product-market fit problem. The thing they'd built was selling and being used, but that fit couldn't support a profitable and growing company.

After some serious conversations, Sam and Devon decided that they needed to move away from their direct-to-consumer approach. But they did not quit. Instead, they looked at what was working. While selling seat licenses to companies for use by employees, they had learned that larger businesses were not happy with their options for travel management software. The gaps those companies were experiencing could be filled by the product Pana had built.

"With our value proposition (exceptional service, seamless travel planning, simple payment, etc.), we had to convince our initial target customer that they had a problem and we could do it better. But our new customer (overworked administrative personnel at large companies) felt this pain intimately, and they were thrilled to find a fix," says Tivona. "Pana became a travel management company for businesses, largely offering its original product but pricing at a level that would be profitable and developing a model that scaled.

"For us, by pivoting the target customer, we went from charging $24.99 a month (for unlimited access) to sometimes grumpy individual consumers to charging $79 *per trip* to corporate customers who were delighted to pay for the value we added."

A few years later, in the middle of a global pandemic, Pana sold itself to software leader Coupa in an accretive transaction.

IMPROVING BRAND AND REACH BY ASSOCIATION

I put myself near superstars. I managed to persuade influential people with significant networks to join some of these escapades like Leadership Camp and forums. Often those people found value. When they did, they mentioned my work to others. I asked them for testimonials. My group of endorsements and logos on my site became broader and more sophisticated. More importantly, my word-of-mouth referral flywheel grew. Today I routinely hear from new prospects who say they heard about my work from someone I don't know. I rarely reveal that fact, but I take great pleasure in noticing the ripples.

PARTNERSHIP WHEN IT SEEMS EITHER ACCRETIVE OR FUN

Many salespeople, and especially sellers who become solopreneurs, prefer the individual experience of winning deals, hitting goals, and building their chunk of the business (or the whole business). They may enjoy doing this in the context of teams, but successful sellers are often extremely self-motivated and favor autonomy over collaboration. For these types of sellers, personal accountability comes with more freedom, even though it also comes with more risk. That said, whether you optimize for independence or collaboration, partnership can be a critical key to winning.

I'm an independent person, but I'm also extremely social. At various points in my life, I've elected to try running an experiment with another person. These efforts haven't always been rip-roaring successes, and when they were not, they were one time only. Because of my work around zone of genius, I know what I like to do in a collaborative project, and I try to ascertain how things will go in advance as well as I can. When I'm wrong, the other person and I usually quite agreeably decide that a given project will not be a recurring one.

Furthermore, I am a big believer in clearly discussing roles and responsibilities among the partners up front. Partner dynamics shift over time, so stay current. In my experience, one of the most important roles in a partnership is selling. If I'm the primary seller of a business with a partner, I will generally structure the relationship so that the others involved are responsible for other meaningful parts of the execution. And when I partner with a great seller, I *am* the one who handles the doing!

PRIORITIZING TIME THROUGH EXTREME DISCERNMENT

Many of you, like many entrepreneurs, are likely reading this and other books as you are running your business. Growth-oriented businesspeople often learn while flying the plane. As such, you already know how precious a resource your time is. I need to be reminded of this often. My reminders usually come in missteps. And I keep trying to nail the balance of how to allocate or "spend" my time given my current goals for each stage of my business life. I encourage you now and on an ongoing basis to audit your time and gain more discernment about where it is best used.

For example, during most of my time as a solopreneur, I've declined meetings with people who do things that overlap with what I do. This bucket of meeting requests is and always has been huge for me. People in my network will meet someone who seems like they have something in common with me, and they'll send a note saying, "You are both executive coaches [or tech people, businesswomen, etc.]. You two should meet." Since I've always had a large influx of meeting requests, I've never understood the value of getting together to talk about someone else's coaching and facilitation business. Part of this is style (remember that independence thing I mentioned?), and part of it is stage (I've been at this a while). This rule won't necessarily be right for you, or it may not be right for you right now; you may draw different lines, especially when you're just getting started.

That said, I do partner with people who I think would be fun or accretive as collaborators, as mentioned previously. I also say yes to meetings requested by close friends asking me to do a favor for someone who matters to them. I almost always take meetings with people who are new to my town of Boulder. If I were just starting out and a seasoned person wanted to meet with me as a potential referral partner, that might be worthwhile. I routinely look at guidelines like these and reevaluate to stay current and intentional.

Your choices may look different, and that's super. The point is to be clear

about where and how you want to spend your discretionary time to ensure
that you are using your most precious resource in alignment with the goals
you have set.

PIVOT. LEARN. EXECUTE. REPEAT.

I routinely evaluate my level of contentment, interest, and energy for my
work in my solopreneur business. I gut check how I'm feeling about different
pieces of work against all the things I asked you to investigate, including core
values, zone of genius, and essence qualities. When I look at the day's calendar, I try to notice whether there is a slot that I'm not looking forward to
or truly wishing to avoid. When I notice those reactions, I ask myself what
is not working in that engagement. I sometimes go broader, asking what
might be off with how I am structuring my work or relating to it. Making
this self-inquiry a consistent part of what I'm doing is critical to the growth
of my business. If I am not deeply engaged in my work, my flywheel of new
business and sales will suffer. It may take years for the effects of my disen-
gagement to manifest themselves, but it will happen.

I invite you to do routine retrospectives on your projects or your clients.
You can try it right now by looking back three to six months in your calendar and following these prompts:

- Check the alignment between what you're doing (or have done) and
  your energy level in hindsight. Were you fired up about that work
  and that client? Did it feel like drudgery? Something in between?
- Pivot in areas where you have the flexibility to become more
  engaged. This may mean pivoting your work, your pace of work,
  your clients, your main contact at one of your clients, your way of
  working, or your mindset around your work.
- Engaging in this process takes discipline. Set a calendar appoint-
  ment for six months hence to ask yourself these questions again
  after you've made some adjustments.
- Recruit (and be) an accountability partner around this exercise to
  ensure that you do it.

===== **EXERCISE** =====
Looking Back with the Gift of Hindsight

Review my principles for getting started and apply the one or two that resonate most with your new or evolving business. Then ask yourself whether there is anything you want to change based on those two principles. These questions may help:

+ Should you tweak either your pricing or your packaging right now to be in better alignment with how things are going?
+ Would you like to run a new experiment in marketing or any other area of your business?
+ Would this be a good time to ask a client or a prospect who turned you down for any feedback on why?
+ What three things could you do today to make your network more productive?
+ Are there any meetings you want to set or cancel?
+ Are there any relationships to projects, clients, or prospects that you'd like to try to adjust?

Once you've answered those questions, take one specific action this week.

PART 5

MARKETING YOU: AUTHENTICALLY, IMPERFECTLY, AND OFTEN

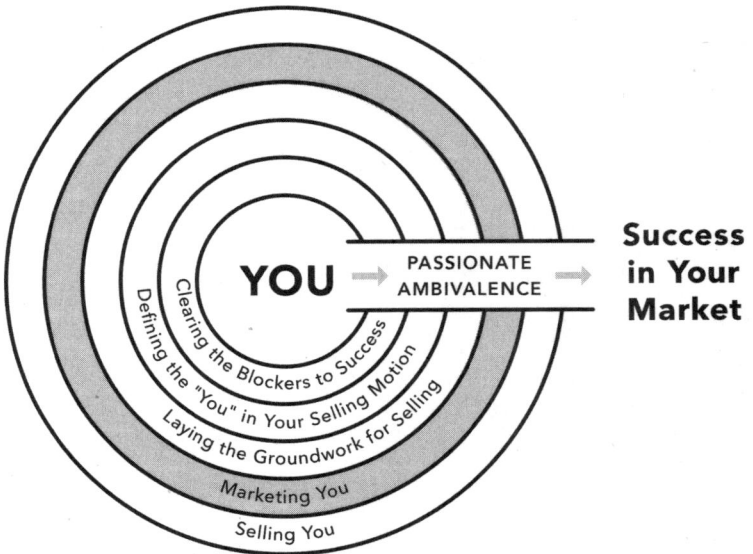

YOU → PASSIONATE AMBIVALENCE → Success in Your Market

Clearing the Blockers to Success
Defining the "You" in Your Selling Motion
Laying the Groundwork for Selling
Marketing You
Selling You

CHAPTER 15

DIGITAL YOU

Y ou have done a lot of heavy lifting. Now it's time to leverage all your inner work and self-awareness and put something out into the world that mirrors the deepest and most compelling version of you. You may be thinking as you read this that *before* you take the next step, you would be wise to know your market, your potential customers, and what those people and organizations want most. I suggest that you ought to stake your ground first with the clarity and authenticity you've just earned and then adjust your pitch if needed based on what you learn from your prospective customers and the market.

Given the choice between crafting a message that centers on you and crafting one that you think will please others, you're better off starting with the former.

For fans of the Netflix series *Bridgerton*, there is a scene in season three, episode two ("How Bright the Moon") in which Colin Bridgerton advises his friend Penelope Featherington on how to find a husband:

Penelope: Shall I pretend to flirt with the imaginary cellist?

Colin: No, with the dashing suitor you just met by the refreshments. Me.

Penelope: You?

Colin: I'm the perfect person to practice on. You don't have to be embarrassed. You know me.

Penelope: That is exactly why I will feel even more embarrassed. I know you.

Penelope: Forgive me, it is only … Deep inside, I know I can be clever and amusing, but somehow, my character gets lost between my heart and my mouth, and I find myself saying the wrong thing or, more likely, nothing at all.

Colin: Forget what is wrong or right. Imagine what you would want to say to me if I were a suitor without concerning yourself with how I might receive it.

That piece of advice—that Penelope should present herself authentically to suitors without any regard for what the suitor would think—is precisely what I want you to keep at the front of your mind. Build a brand that is uniquely, authentically, radically about you, even if that is improper by Regency-era standards. You and Penelope are worthy of suitors (for you, clients or customers), but you need to focus less on what others think and more on allowing your true self to shine.

I recommend that you craft all your messaging in every digital place you inhabit, ensuring that everything you share is consistent with what you have learned so far. You and your business are intimately intertwined. The public presentation of you and the presentation of your business should be just as close.

Here are the places where you must share your story about you and the key focus of your business as soon as possible. In my view, perfect is the enemy of more than the good. It is the enemy of getting started, learning, experimenting, and iterating. Put something out there, start to receive responses, and commit to constant iteration.

NAME AND LOGO

You must have a name for your company that embodies you and what you are up to in your business. To do that, you should have a decent website domain address, a name that is not a gross infringement of someone else's trademark, and a logo that looks professional enough to meet the expectations of your market. You need not use a marketing and branding agency for this project unless your market demands it. Why? Because everything you're doing is a constant experiment. Overinvesting at the start will undermine your strategy of continual learning. Launch with something good enough, and get smarter and more aligned from there.

You may choose to use a version of your personal name, optionally adding another word ("services," "consultants," "resources," etc.). Sounds great. Just be sure when you make this decision that it aligns with how "big" you want your company to seem and one day be. If you imagine having a raft of employees at some point, think about that when naming your business after yourself. As you make these choices, look at a few businesses with which you might compete to obtain an idea of what you like and dislike about how comparable businesses are presented online. Once you settle on your logo, ask a designer to craft a mini–"style guide" for your preferred fonts, colors, and core elements of your brand, as shown in the following mini–style guide.

Branding my company has been a journey for me, and it may evolve for you as well. I started my company a decade ago under the name Boulder Ideas. I live in Boulder, Colorado. I liked the play between the words "Boulder" and "bolder," and this name seemed like a vehicle that could appear larger than me if I wanted to create that perception or enact that reality. After a few years, I started to see that my decades of experience in business, combined with my odd and Googleable last name, suggested that I pivot to making my business just…me. I rehoused the website and all related materials under SueHeilbronner.com. A few years into that decision, I got so fed up with my last name (which I've never much liked as a Jewish person of German heritage) that I scoured the domain registries for simple domains that used .com (as opposed to, for example, .co or .biz or .us) and incorporated the word "sue." This wasn't easy because domains are taken or priced in accordance with market demand, and "sue-ing" someone is a lucrative legal activity. I considered "cuesue.com," "truesue.com," and more. They were available but too cute. Late one night, I contacted the owner of HeySue.com. She was using the domain to redirect to another domain, and her business sold dinosaur-related toys. Thirty minutes, four emails, and $1,000 later, I

HeySue.com Branding

It Looks
Warm
Inviting
Sophisticated

It Feels
Approachable
Friendly
Conversational

Color Palette

Slate Blue	Electric Blue	Stone Blue	Green
HEX #313E4D	HEX #00B6E3	HEX #10525F	HEX #9ECB3A

Logo Treatments

Full Color Horizontal

Full Color Horizontal + Name

Knockout Horizontal on Stone Blue

Knockout Horizontal + Name on Stone Blue

Full Color Vertical

Full Color Vertical + Name

Knockout Vertical on Stone Blue

Knockout Vertical + Name on Stone Blue

Typography

The chosen typeface for the body copy is Roboto and Zilla Slab for headings. This will work well across digital platforms and can be used easily with Google Fonts.

Roboto Regular   **Roboto Bold**   Roboto Medium

Zilla Slab Regular   **Zilla Slab Semibold**

PARAGRAPH
Sue Heilbronner is a conscious leadership coach, team facilitator, keynote speaker, and author. She has worked with global companies like Meta, Google, Salesforce, Gainsight, Oracle, and more.

HEADINGS
Heading 1 - 64pt/64
Heading 2 - 48pt/64
Heading 3 - 32pt/36
Heading 4 - 20pt/28

owned the best domain I could imagine. It feels like me. My email address is sue@heysue.com. I have a way of saying this that involves play and pointing.

Ten years. Three names. I think this will be my last one.

The estimated cost for the step of naming your business and basic design guidance for your company ought to be no more than $2,000 and could be far less if you use crowdsourced or AI-powered design resources. The one mandatory expense is your domain registration, which will usually be $15 per year (at the time of writing) for an available (unregistered) domain. You can choose your own colors, design usable logos on your own or using an AI design tool, and search USPTO.gov and the web in general for possible trademark conflicts. If you're planning on going big, this last piece is important, and I suggest that you find a trademark lawyer to advise you on whether to use or register a new mark. A small trademark firm will save you money on this front and be fine for handling this task.

KEY BRAND ELEMENTS

Now revisit the top two core values that you identified earlier, and use those and the other work you've done to identify any elements that are inextricably linked to your brand and the way you intend to work.

To give you an idea of the elements that may belong in this bucket—which will extend to how you present yourself to the world and to potential clients—here are a few of mine and how I use them in practice.

I did a prospect call just yesterday for a 1:1 coaching engagement with a C-level leader at a major hospitality brand. We were getting to know each other. I was giving him a sense of what it might be like to work with me by getting to know him in my typical style. I asked **direct and pointed questions**. That's one of my key brand elements.

He went on to share some thoughts on a tendency he has toward humility, and he connected that tendency to his religious faith. We had been on this first call for six minutes. I quickly let him know that I curse with some regularity and that I'm Jewish. I asked if that felt comfortable for him. He said yes. **Using authentic revealing** to determine fit and chemistry is one of my key brand elements.

Finally, I told him that working with me might be uncomfortable at times, and the discomfort would hopefully be of service in the long run. I said I was likely to push him in areas that I believed offered growth opportunities. I was clear that **loving challenge instead of soothing comfort** is one of my key brand elements.

There's one more I adopted a few years into working as a solopreneur. I stopped wearing proper business attire, and **I decided that I would work only with clients who would be fine if I showed up wearing sneakers.** If you're in tech and you're a guy reading this in a hoodie, you may think that's no big deal. If you're a woman of a certain age who charges an awful lot of coin to work at fancy companies, as I am, it was a meaningful decision to stand for a key element of my brand.

My brand elements come with me in most of what I write about, say about myself, share with prospects, and offer in my work.

=== **EXERCISE** ===
Your Brand Elements

Identify two to three "brand elements" that you haven't covered in core values or zone of genius and that you would be willing to stand for in your work.

WEBSITE

About two years into running my company, I was ambling around a Target store, and I got a call from someone I didn't know. He was the CFO of a religious Christian homeschooling company. The company generated materials and curricula for homeschooling families. He told me the company was forming a new division. It was creating a secular homeschooling company, leveraging decades of experience in the sector and relationships with public school officials to reach parents who were not religious or who wanted their homeschooled kids to have a secular education.

I will never forget that phone call. The caller was the head of this new entity, and he said, "I feel like I need someone rebellious and irreverent to give me the courage and outside point of view to push through a project that is new for this company's DNA." I thought, *Wait, you want someone rebellious and irreverent?* I knew I was these things. But how did this stranger know that? Well, he read my website, my blog posts, and my social media posts. All those places, directly or indirectly, made this stranger think I was his person. This, my friends, is beautiful. I was hired at our first meeting. We jointly named the new business and did all the branding and website development. Together.

It is imperative that you show up as you on your site and every other public venue.

How do you make sure you do that? Your website. If you have one, look at it anew, considering everything we covered in the previous chapters. If you're beginning fresh, you have a running start from the exercises that precede this chapter.

On your site, tell your story and the story of the business you're engaged in using exactly the voice, spirit, humor, brand elements, and language of YOU. Being with your site should feel like being with you. These words really matter, not just because of what people will think when they visit your site but because search engines are also paying attention. Of course, you should learn enough about search engine optimization (SEO) to implement the basics. But in general, you should be confident that a high-quality, honest recitation of what your business does and who you are will be fine. My favorite SEO resource is Search Engine Roundtable, run by the famous and hyperethical Schwartz brothers. If you're the target audience for this book, you aren't generating heaps of sales leads from Google searches. You are planning to be out in the world, doing amazing work, and getting leads from people who know you or work with you and recommend you to others.

Still, your website will be motivating and clarifying for you and others. So do the work. Take some time. In addition, you will likely be shocked to find that every now and then, someone will reach out to you after having read your site in its entirety. They will contact you because they want to work with YOU. Those are great days.

If you're just getting started, find someone (or jump in yourself) to build a highly editable, mobile-enabled website on Webflow, WordPress, Wix,

Squarespace, or another content management system you like. Regardless of whether you or another resource builds your site, be sure that it's built on a user-friendly content management system, which you'll find on the platforms I mentioned previously. This way, you can keep up with 90 percent of the content edits you'll want on your site yourself.

To lay the groundwork for yourself or a web designer you hire, you'll want to knock out a few basic tasks.

EXERCISE
Your Site Basics

+ Find five sites you love that fit the look and feel of what you're after. Jot down three to five things about each site that you would like to emulate. Grab screenshots. It is helpful to pick sites of smaller companies or solopreneurs, which are more likely to be achievable at reasonable expense.
+ Write copy for what you view as the mission-critical pages (or sections) of a basic business website.
  » Home page
  » About me (or us)
  » My work
  » Current and past clients/testimonials
  » Blog overview page, if you want a blog
  » Contact form

+ Gather one or two photos of you, including shots of you working, to use on the home page, the about page, and in other appropriate locations.
+ Share a structure and design ideas with a designer (which could be you) and start building. A reasonable first draft is a good first step.
+ Ask a few friends or allies to share their feedback.

Your first site build should take no more than one month if you do the work on drafting site copy and visual asset collection. If you hire someone to do the design and development, the total cost of your first site should be no more than $4,000. If you are selling something expensive, you can go to $6,000 with the addition of a few clever bits of functionality or visual imagery. You can pay more. You can pay less. As of the date of this writing, I believe these amounts will suffice for what you need at this stage. If your favorite cousin does the work, I hope you will pay less. If you hire an agency, you will likely pay more, and I don't think you need that added expense at the start. You should expect to have ongoing hosting fees and perhaps a monthly retainer for updates by your site developer.

You'll get bored with hearing me say this, but don't waste your time shooting for perfection on your first attempt. **Get. Something. Live.** It will advance your progress toward your goals. Iterate from there. Obtain compelling, current head shots. Find free or licensable photography or video that resonates with you and your messaging. Unsplash offers royalty-free photos. Getty and iStock offer reasonable packages for imagery. There is a wealth of free and paid AI imagery tools you might try. Use those tools to create a site that a visitor can feel even if they don't read it. Make your message land in less than one second using visual excellence.

TESTIMONIALS

An additional requirement for a compelling business presence is a collection of qualified endorsements, preferably from at least one recognizable logo or company. Find a way to secure a few testimonials from people who have worked with you, even if it was at a large company where you worked before starting your solopreneur venture. If you're early in your career and you were, say, a teaching assistant for a great professor at your college, ask that professor for a testimonial. Even if the testimonials are general (because, perhaps, this thing you're doing is new for you), collect testimonials that allude to your intellect, passion, clarity, or public speaking ability. Anything you can get at the start will help. Look at LinkedIn for old recommendations you probably forgot. Of course, you must ask for explicit permission to use a testimonial in a public context—on your site, in social media, in a proposal, or in your email signature.

As you progress in your business, keep asking for testimonials. This may seem awkward at first, but you need to pay attention to these opportunities so that when you get them, they feel authentic. I like testimonials of about twenty words. I might use the entire testimonial in long-form environments (like a website testimonials page) and a shorter portion for pithier purposes.

I was invited to present at the Conscious Entrepreneurs Summit in Boulder, Colorado. I asked my friend Vlada Bortnik, cofounder and CEO of Marco Polo, if she would allow me to interview her at this event. She said yes. Hooray! I chose this path because I *love* interviewing people onstage.

After the session, people came up to me, the lowly interviewer, and praised my interviewing skills. One person said it was the perfect interview because it was like listening to a live coaching session. This was one of our goals for the session! A few others gave lengthy and specific praise highlighting features of that interview that made me proud. I thought about the experience that night, and I realized that conference organizers generally put too little emphasis on the interviewers. There is far more focus on the speaker, but a speaker showcased by a lousy interviewer looks boring. I had a realization that instead of just being a keynote speaker now and then, I could promote myself as a keynote *interviewer* and market the benefits to companies and conferences of creating the most authentic, provocative, vulnerable, and fresh interviews of speakers that their audiences would ever experience.

That night, I emailed two of the people (with senior roles and significant companies, because the status of endorsement providers matters) who had appreciated my efforts and asked them for attributable testimonials for my new landing page promoting me as a keynote interviewer. The next day, I received this from a dear friend:

> Sue's interviews are nothing short of captivating. Her potent blend of humor, insightful questions, and unique content keeps you riveted. For once, the interviewer shines as brightly as the interviewee in effortlessly creating an incredibly compelling conversation. I wouldn't think twice about investing in an opportunity to witness her electrify any dialogue—she's a true game-changer in this role.

That is how you get a testimonial in the best way possible. This is also how you can spin up a new product or new positioning in your zone of genius almost overnight. You listen to what people are saying as they appreciate your work (even if it's noncustomer work), and you ask them if they would be willing to give you something you can use. Once you have a few testimonials, keep refreshing them and your "most impressive logo" section of "current and past customers" on your home page. This has a very meaningful impact on how you are perceived.

Here is a quick checklist for testimonials:

- Ask people who tell you things casually if you can use what they just told you or something else as a testimonial.
- Confirm that you can use not only the text of the statement but also the name and title of the person.
- Target twenty-word testimonials.
- Use testimonials on your site, relevant social media accounts, proposals, email signature, or other marketing materials.
- Prioritize testimonials with great content or from well-respected people in your field.
- Routinely refresh your testimonials for currency.

Once you have the first iteration of these key features of your site, go live.

LINKEDIN AND OTHER, LESS IMPORTANT SOCIAL MEDIA SITES

I cannot emphasize this enough: Ensure that you and your voice are positioned in a way that feels sales-positive everywhere on the web. Go. Do this now. If you haven't updated your LinkedIn profile since your first job out of college, put this book down and get it done. If you haven't written a LinkedIn headline that sells you in just your style, go fix that. If your picture is lousy and doesn't look compelling (would you ask that person if they are available for a project like the projects you are marketing?), change it. Is there bias in what people think about LinkedIn profiles? Yes. There is. So give yourself the very best shot by ensuring that you present yourself as well as you can. If people reject that, so be it.

After you've made those edits to LinkedIn, make sure you are connected to every single person you know whom you regard as a decent human being. Reach out for connections. Every time you have a meeting with a company you respect, ask for connections to everyone you meet. If you have a prospect call, connect to that person. If you have a prospect call that doesn't go anywhere, connect to that person. I do not think I'm the only person on the planet who makes surface judgments about a person based on the quality of their LinkedIn network. Actually, I know I'm not, because a CEO once hired me on the first call and commented, "Well, I can see how successful you must be based on the number of well-positioned people in your network." If you're not a person of a certain age who might have been an early member of LinkedIn, this is even more pressing. Connect with your parents' friends who are decent humans, too.

Now, this gets a little spicier when thinking of other social media platforms. I do not recommend turning all your personal profiles on Facebook, Instagram, Twitter/X, and others into marketing avenues. It likely won't work, although I know many very successful influencer-driven businesses have been built on those platforms. What I do recommend is cultivating a good network of friends and connections that make sense based on the sites you like to use. Amplify the voices of people you think are worth amplifying so you are putting some pennies in the karma jar. Publish authentic shares when you want to, as you normally would, but perhaps with slightly more regularity so you're on people's minds.

Then, when it's time to post about a kid's graduation or an Easter-egg hunt, do that. But remember, when you post about an egg hunt, you are the person who runs this kind of business who likes kids looking for eggs. This shouldn't be a big reach because you will have done all the work I've recommended to ensure that you're showing up in all areas of your life *as you*. Just remember that personal and business are intertwined even more for solopreneurs.

If you do all these things, dear reader, every once in a great while, your network will give you permission to share a post that advances a particularly interesting or important area of your work or your company. These chances are golden. Be casual, offhanded, and intentional. Use a great visual (that matters a ton). Tease the idea of something amazing you're doing and, even better, someone amazing who's your customer for this amazing thing.

I use LinkedIn constantly. I am on Facebook with some regularity. I use Twitter/X less regularly. Every year, my collaborator Kaley Klemp and I run a six-month program called Certification for Leader Coaches. I post about this program once on each of these platforms with a strong visual. I say something like

> This program designed for working leaders who want to bring more coaching into their leadership is happening again in 2026. We have a few seats left for stellar, self-aware leaders. This program has sold out every time it's been offered well in advance. If you want to chat about whether it's a fit for you or someone on your team, DM me. If you want to jump that step and apply, apply here.

That one post generates two to three participants each year at a value of $15,000 per attendee. One free post offered authentically in the context of an avid, intentional, supportive social media context.

Some of you will be prioritizing more "social" sites in addition to LinkedIn. If your business relies heavily on social influencing, you may focus on Instagram or Threads. Many of the same principles apply in that context.

DON'T SPAM OR OVERPROMOTE

What I most definitely do not recommend is spamming your LinkedIn feed for a specific offering. Post once and sometimes twice about something you're offering. Ask a few people to like one of your important posts so it gets boosted by the LinkedIn algorithm, but I don't suggest posting every day or every few hours for months about something on the horizon. I hold the belief that by overpromoting a premium offering, you degrade your brand and the perceived quality of the offering. You don't want to seem desperate. You want to seem selective. You don't want to offer a different discount every week. You want your price to stand on its own as reasonably well cor-related with what you're putting out in the world. I don't know that I'm right about this, but my beliefs represent facets of passionate ambivalence in an indirect sales context.

BLOGGING, EMAIL UPDATES, NEWSLETTERS, AND SEO

Blogging

I blog. I've done videos. I've run a "channel" on the Marco Polo video chat app. I've hosted a podcast for years. Nothing has been as pleasurable to me as blogging. Sometimes I write about conscious leadership or a new lesson in business; now and then I've posted a screed on, say, cargo shorts. During my many years of blogging, I've been unconsciously committed to *not* writing a long-form book, and blogging felt easier because of the lower barrier to entry. I blog on my site using the tool that is part of the Webflow content management system. I have a connection between Webflow and Mailchimp, which is my email list tool.

Email List

You should decide whether you want to create content to support your sell-ing effort. The options are many—from an occasional LinkedIn or Insta-gram post to a daily blog or weekly podcast. Most experts will say what you have likely observed as a consumer: The goal of content generation is build-ing an audience. That could be a social media following. My most valuable avenue for awareness is my opt-in email list. If you want to create content, I recommend that you set up an email distribution plan. Create a small target list of people who you know will be happy to hear from you, ensure that your email program is legally compliant (all major tools do this), create a modal on your website to invite site visitors to opt in to your list, connect your opt-in tool to your email program, and start creating and distributing content good enough that people will stay with you and recommend your blog posts, videos, or newsletters to others. When you write a blog post, you'll also want to be sure to post it to relevant social media platforms to increase visibility. If a blog with a newsletter feels like a bridge too far, you can gain decent traction from writing excellent posts on social media and performing the other actions I recommend to bolster your presence on the platforms you choose.

My opt-in list has been valuable, even though it has stayed largely stable at one thousand people. Aside from the direct sales conversion that happens through this flow, my audience and my future audience learn how I think about things through my blog. When I receive inbound emails about possible work from people to whom I'm not connected (pure web leads), I ask them to look at my site and my blog and let me know what makes them feel like I may be a fit for them. I like giving cold leads a small homework assignment to qualify them a bit, and this exact exercise helps them commit to how we might be a fit even before we have a conversation.

SEO

One additional benefit I gain from blogging is SEO. I won't spend a bunch of time talking about how to do great SEO, because I don't really "do" SEO. Instead, I try to do what I advised you to do with your website—craft high-quality, current content on my blog and, of course, keep my website up-to-date. Quality is the most important thing for SEO, so I'm checking that box. I also optimize for certain keyword phrases that matter to me. I rarely use the term "coach" without the word "executive" in front of it, for example. That's a matter of branding and a matter of SEO, and if you look at my site and my blog posts, you'll see clear themes that I emphasize because they may drive qualified prospects to my site from a search. It's a base-covering approach. I recently blogged about the pros and cons of securing a coaching certification. I have strong views on this, and people regularly ask my opinion. I wrote the blog post to have something to give people who ask my opinion (again, avoiding a phone call). But I *also* run a coaching certification program, so a post like this can instigate sales. You could do more, and if you want to, there's plenty to read on this topic.

More Social (Less Business) Social Media Tools

I mention blogging and email because these have been great strategies for me. However, the trend toward influencer marketing that focuses on less business-oriented social sites (and frankly some business sites) is growing. If tools like YouTube, Instagram, or podcasting sync well with your talents, your audience, and your business offering, these are massive connection points that are relatively easy to test. I am not an expert, but simple research on YouTube about the topic of marketing through YouTube will prove productive if video is a tool that makes sense for you.

TESTING, TESTING

I want to emphasize that, as in many other areas of your selling strategy, content creation and marketing are experimental. Sure, you'll want to lean in first to the places where you have the most talent and interest and where you think your customer is most likely to find you and engage with your content. But you won't know that in advance of trying things out. Approach this piece of selling with a testing mindset.

As you're testing, be sure you're measuring the impact of your tests. If you write a blog post, create a social post, or record and release a podcast, evaluate which effort garnered the most positive feedback from the market. This may be likes, emails or texts, shares, list growth, inbound sales inquiries, or growth in the number of followers. While you're testing, remember to consider whether the content you've created gives you something you can use in a sales conversation. That is an added value.

Continue to refine your digital strategy based on what you learn, what works, what you like, and what is emerging in a rapidly changing landscape.

EXERCISE
Prioritize Your Digital Strategy

+ Write a list of what you want to create, and rank these initiatives in priority order.
+ Decide whether you want to be a content creator (or hire one) to support your sales efforts. If yes, decide which content you think you are best suited to create based on the intersection of your own interests and talent and what you believe your target customer would most appreciate.
+ Create a schedule for your content creation. Start small, perhaps setting a deadline for the development of your first three pieces of content.
+ Decide where you will initially be distributing your content.
+ Decide how you will measure the success of your content efforts and define what "success" looks like for your early efforts.

CHAPTER 16

SHOWING UP AND MAKING AN IMPACT

There is a wide range of nonquantifiable marketing that I generally classify as "showing up and trying to be a decent contributor." The Techstars startup accelerator was founded in Boulder. The team there began using the phrase "#givefirst" to represent a community-forward mindset of giving without any expectation of getting anything back. I think this is a remarkable concept.

I will propose a few examples of things you can do that fall into my bucket of "showing up," but you likely will have ideas for your own context in your work or your community. Follow your intuition. The extent to which you put yourself out there as a decent, valuable person in the area where you can generate business will serve you well, even if it takes time. People notice people who make contributions. They talk about those people. The more people are talking about you, the more likely it is that a conversation will happen between someone who is looking for someone like you and someone who has seen you showing up.

WALKING-AROUND-TOWN MARKETING

When I moved to Boulder, I was enveloped by other people sharing their #givefirst love, energy, and opportunities. I don't recall that I made a major outreach effort, but somehow I had coffee dates or random collisions with the dean and the entrepreneurship professor at the University of Colorado Law School. That led to a stint as an adjunct professor of entrepreneurship. I was able to become a mentor at Techstars, a volunteer position that gave me a chance to meet entrepreneurs, investors, and other amazing humans from the area.

I took every chance I got to participate in Boulder Startup Week and TEDxBoulder, two very successful volunteer-driven events led by Andrew Hyde, who is committed to #givefirst. I showed up for infinite networking events, panels, meetups, and more. I'm not sure I did this to promote anything, but I know that my presence helped me establish a place in the ecosystem. Three years later, when I founded my executive coaching and consulting company, that resonance worked in my favor. And I didn't stop. I made almost no direct asks in my small city. I simply enjoyed the benefit of what this walking-around-town marketing can do to embellish one's brand.

I took many, many pick-your-brain meetings as part of my efforts to #givefirst. I spoke about this and the Booth earlier in this book. It has served me. If you have the time, #givefirst. If you have more time, #givemore.

STAY CURRENT

Another suggestion about marketing outside your digital brand presentation: Stay current. I mean this in two different ways.

First, stay apprised of macroconditions that affect your industry and places where you work. This is particularly important if you choose to engage in social media marketing or write blog posts. Be aware of the top headlines locally, nationally, and internationally. Don't be the obtuse seller who posts about some pricey offering on a day when the stock market falls off a cliff. Staying abreast of the news can also be helpful in the ongoing work of refining your brand and business offerings. You will be better able to spot new projects or even circle back to an idea that didn't succeed under the conditions of your first attempt. Generalized awareness of the political, economic, and personal news around you keeps you nimble, thinking creatively about all the ways the world needs you and your superb talents.

Second, stay current with your network. Don't be cheesy, overbearing, or, heaven forbid, salesy, but stay abreast of what the people you respect are up to. I read the local newspaper (digitally), so I know about these things. Sure, I may see this stuff on the socials, but I won't miss it if I read the Boulder *Daily Camera*. When you are scanning media sources, notice other people's posts that are questions, requests for help, or interest in introductions, and add value where you can. Make useful introductions, try out a new product or service yourself, or promote something you find valuable to others who may be able to use it. And when someone in your network or town does something amazing, publicly celebrate them, raising the visibility of their achievement. If this is not second nature for you, make a point weekly of finding one or two areas across your network where you can be additive. And be additive.

MAKE DIRECT, PERSONAL ASKS WHEN IT MAKES SENSE

Finally, once you've done all you can to ensure that almost everyone on the planet one degree of separation from you knows what you're up to and what you're looking for to build your business, I urge you to make direct, personal asks when it makes sense. If you just read that sentence and felt your stomach tighten, you are not alone. However, it's imperative that you understand that passionate ambivalence does *not* mean that you are off the hook about being vulnerable in reaching out to your family, close friends, colleagues, past colleagues, close social media connections, mentors, investors, recruitment people at search firms you've worked with, and more to let them know that your shingle is officially up. Let them know, preferably individually, that you are interested in meeting great prospects (perhaps including that very person you're reaching out to) for the product or service you are selling.

None of the more wink-wink-nudge-nudge efforts I discuss in this marketing section will work if you don't light the fuse that's right in front of you—your close connections. I recently spoke with a former client who left his VP role in tech to start a coaching business. He has a newish podcast; he blogs every week; he has a LinkedIn newsletter; he is all over social media advancing the interests of people he values. The flywheel isn't working yet, and he's giving himself six more months of runway to see if it might start turning. I asked, "Have you made direct asks about working with you to people who know you about hiring you?" I could hear his head hang down to his chest in his tone. "No, not yet," he said. It had been six months.

In my investing days, I often asked new founders whether they had asked any friends or family to invest in the new venture. I know that not everyone has friends or family who *can* invest in a startup, but I asked. Many founders said they hadn't because it felt too vulnerable to put themselves out there with people they knew. I understand this feeling for founders and new solopreneurs, but it is imperative to make those asks. There are two reasons. First, those people should be your closest path to a close (of a new client or a startup investment). Second, if you're not willing to ask qualified people close to you to invest in you or work with you, you don't have enough confidence in what you're doing to earn a stranger's business.

EXERCISE
Power Your Flywheel

You've read about some tactics that I crafted or stumbled upon that helped power my flywheel in the early days. That flywheel continues to hum ten years later. What is *your version* of these kinds of activities that work for you, given your network, type of work, interests, zone of genius, and target audience? Think of things that you can test. Commit to two next actions with a timeline.

CHAPTER 17

KNOWING YOUR BEST PROSPECT

E verything we have covered so far is focused on you knowing you. Now we are going to discuss the concept of the ideal customer profile (ICP).

YOUR ICP

Just thinking about your ICP and being intentional in vetting prospects and opportunities should be of great value to you. When a prospect matches your ICP, they are more likely to choose you, and you are more likely to have a successful engagement at a price at which you're happy. To get your wheels turning, here's a definition of my ICP, which covers individuals, teams, and companies.

- They are in a for-profit business that already has some traction in the form of material revenue or fundraising (i.e., they can afford my premium rates).
- They are in a business that is associated with or directly reliant on technology.
- They are not in a "vice" space such as guns, tobacco, lotteries, etc.
- They are very focused on personal growth, and they believe that personal growth drives positive business outcomes.

- They are low on process and high on trust. They move quickly.
- They are authentic and willing to be vulnerable early.
- They are game to experiment and try new things; they are not stuck in old patterns that they want to preserve because "it's just the way it is."
- They are game to give and receive consistent feedback, believing in feedback as a driver of high performance.
- They are willing to meet in person some but not all the time we are working together.
- They are in touch with their emotions and believe that emotions are acceptable at work.
- They are good human beings.

These ICP criteria are broad but clarifying. They were looser when I started my company, booking any business I could sell. Now I actively use these criteria to vet prospective clients and to determine where to spend my time on marketing.

EXCEPTIONS AND NON-ICPS

The qualities of my ICP are not fixed; exceptions happen. For example, I work on at least one substantial engagement with a nonprofit I care about each year for free or at materially reduced rates. I also at times work with someone outside my ICP if a current ICP client or dear friend asks me to. These are reasonable decisions for me because I am not expending much effort cultivating the new business. It's largely delivered to me with a warm introduction, and that's usually an easy mutual yes in part as a means to enhance my relationship with the referrer.

But I'm cautious about this. The reason? It is often not in my zone of genius. Earlier in my business (and maybe in yours), I said yes more often, but as I have refined a sense of my zone of genius, I have refined a sense of my ICP. I choose to focus on engagements with the right customers at optimal price points where I can make a meaningful impact. Those factors are usually tied to my ICP. So when presented with a non-ICP situation that isn't through a meaningful connection, I usually politely decline or refer that business to someone else in my network. I know that a bad fit with my ICP often produces suboptimal results in the work and in my happiness.

WHEN TO REVISIT AND REFINE YOUR ICP

I recommend that you think about your ICP deeply now and once every six months or so hereafter to ensure that you are engaging in marketing activities (writ large) that meet your prospective customers where they are, whether digitally or IRL. The story of Devon Tivona and Sam Felsenthal and their company Pana in Chapter 14 is a story of moving a company ICP from individual consumer user priced per month to corporate user priced per trip. The product stayed the same; the customer target shifted. The utility of the product to the refined ICP increased geometrically, along with revenue and performance delivery.

My suggestion to revisit your ICP every six months and not more or less is based on two beliefs. First, you don't want to be obsessed with this because if you do all the right things, your prospects will find you. Second, do it at least every six months because your prospect profile or ICP will change, along with your pricing, as you grow your business. For me, this happened somewhat organically, but in case it's not happening organically for you, take this hint and gut check your ICP.

Many features of a prospective customer are highly specific to the product or service you are offering. If you are in sales for an existing company, you likely have a marketing department that has shared one or two personas of an ideal customer as a targeting device. If you are a startup looking to pitch investors, you hopefully have done a considerable amount of research to find investors who are interested in companies like yours and founders like you. If you haven't, you should.

EXERCISE
Your ICP Criteria

+ List at least five criteria of your ICP.
+ Look at your current funnel of prospects. How many are your ICP? Do you want to act on non-ICP prospects or adjust your ICP?
+ If you want to take action on non-ICP prospects or customers, what is one next step you want to take for each of those accounts?

CHAPTER 18

HOW REFERRALS CAN FUEL YOUR GROWTH

One of the fastest shortcuts that superb people can create on the marketing front is the establishment of referral relationships with qualified referral sources. As your business grows, you can achieve far greater scale and generate passive income by becoming one of those referral sources for other practitioners.

SCALING SOLO

You can gain enormous benefits—economic and lifestyle—from running a business that depends largely on you. But there is at least one major downside to this strategy: You are one person, and you do not scale all that well. I am a 1:1 coach. I facilitate executive team meetings. I run Leadership Camps and programs like Certification for Leader Coaches. I lead sessions for large companies on leadership. I occasionally am a keynote speaker or interviewer for very large audiences at conferences.

In these roles, ordered in the way I have listed them, I have incrementally more scale. However, I am not currently as scalable as a software product. If I suddenly become the "it" thing, my business generally depends on my presence, and I can't scale to infinity.

One way I add scale to my business (and help make several talented people even more successful) is to refer business to others. Referrals with associated referral fees like the ones I'm about to describe are not legal in every industry. Check the appropriate rules for yours. They are A-okay in my line of work.

CULTIVATING PARTNERS

If I am extremely busy, if my revenue looks pretty good for the year, if I am about to take a two-week vacation to Antarctica, if I am too expensive for a prospective client, if my personality is a poor fit with the personality of a person or a company that is in contact with me, if I am not all that interested in what a prospective client is looking for, or if the work a prospective client wants is not in my zone of genius, I generally refer their business to one of my partners. My partners are listed at www.HeySue.com/partners.

I've cultivated my group of partners by seeing each of these people in action. I know their backgrounds. I have a sense of their interests and strengths. I know their personalities, so I can feel where a great fit might happen. I keep up with their price parameters so I can make economically optimized referrals when they arise.

I keep referral deals simple. If I refer business to a referral partner, I ask that they pay me 20 percent of their revenue from that client for a period of two years from the first referral. If that client refers my referral partner to additional clients, fantastic. The referral partner owns 100 percent of that business. I don't use contracts for referral partners. They are people in my trusted inner circle. I'm a lapsed lawyer who generally avoids reading contracts, so I almost never suggest writing them.

DEVELOP A REFERRAL SYSTEM

There are two critical components that make or break a referral system.

1. Your referral partners must be superb. Their quality of work ultimately reflects on you. In addition, if your referral partner is superb, they are likely to keep and grow the business you've

referred to them. That, my friends, is great for customers, and it means more passive income for you. That is scale.

2. Your referral partners must be good at sales. If they are not, you are referring valuable prospects to a dead end. That's bad for your prospect, and it's bad for you. If you get to a point of referring business to others, keep track of whether the deals you send out are closing. Keep track of the prices they are closing at (if your referral partner charges too little, that hurts you both). Keep track of when your referral partners are doing fit calls and failing to close a referred prospect. Qualified prospects are gold. If a referral partner can't close on an engagement, you can't afford to refer business to them.

RUN A GREAT REFERRAL BUSINESS

One challenging feature of running a referral business is that most people who reach out will want to work with *you*. There's an art to teeing up these setups in your referral network. To run a great referral business, keep the following issues in mind:

- Field incoming leads that look credible but may not be good fits for you by adding a qualification exercise that helps you learn more about them and their needs. Kaley Klemp, on whose referrals I grew my business in the early years, uses a questionnaire for any incoming prospect who is looking for a 1:1 coach. She asks ten questions about what a prospect is looking for, and from their answers, she gets a decent feel for who might work as a great referral if she's not in a position to take the business herself.

- Kaley responds to the prospect and says she isn't available for this kind of work, but based on the answers to the questionnaire, she knows that one of her referral partners might be an incredible fit. She then lists a few reasons she believes this is true. She follows that with a paragraph about her appreciation for that partner to *bolster the status* of the partner. This helps address the wingman handoff problem. She then asks the prospect if they would like an introduction.

◆ The referral partner closes the business at a high rate of success. You, the referring party, track the close rates of your partners to optimize the passive revenue garnered through the work you have done.

Remember, generating qualified prospects is the trailing indicator of a massive amount of work you have done, involving every step in this book so far *and* usually being superb at your work in a way that generates word-of-mouth referrals. You want to monetize that effort and reputation, either by doing the work yourself, hiring people to do that work as part of your business, or generating passive income through a referral business.

Figuring out the most appropriate referral structure took some time. When Jim and Diana formed the CLG, I was officially a coach on that team. This was great. Two of the three authors who had written *The 15 Commitments of Conscious Leadership* were generating good buzz and good incoming leads. I would receive referrals from them, and often I closed those deals.

This worked for a year or two early in my business. However, as I became more comfortable with my work and as my network got wind of it, I started generating a lot of my own business. CLG's referral fee was between 40 and 50 percent of my revenue at the time. That referral fee no longer made sense for me when I could generate my own work more regularly. I offered to pay a lower referral fee, but that created misalignment across CLG's coaching ranks. Jim, Diana, and I decided jointly that I would leave the CLG coaching team and focus exclusively on my solopreneur practice. That was a hard and mutual decision for me and the leaders of CLG. But it was the right decision, and making it in a timely fashion preserved very meaningful relationships and materially increased my gross margins. Kaley's referral structure was (and remains) the same as mine is now. She continues to refer business to me to this day.

For me, and perhaps for you, getting these referral relationships right is an ongoing process that depends on your economics at the time. In this chapter of my business, paying 20 percent when I am not fully booked feels great to me.

Paying referral fees is like paying taxes. I never *love* making payments—which often are substantial—but I know that referral payments correspond directly to my success. It's a privilege to pay them.

═══ EXERCISE ═══
Lay the Groundwork for Your Referral Business

1. For you to benefit as a recipient of referrals, you want to identify who your referring partners might be. These people are doing something akin to what you're doing or something tangential to what you're doing such that your product or service might complement work they are already doing with clients.

   • Write down a list of potential referrers that are direct competitors, doing what you want to be doing or something quite close.
   • Write down a list of potential referrers who are doing something tangential, where your work might add even more value for their customers.
   • Some of the people or companies on your list may be known to you, and some may not. Create a customized email for each person or company that lets them know what you're up to and invites a conversation to learn more about whether you might be a strong working partner (for complementary work) or referral partner (for similar work) for them.
   • Have the conversation with anyone who agrees to have it, and endeavor to find ways to solidify your partnership through a placement on their partner page, a formal referral agreement, or a test project or introduction with a potential referral client.

2. Create a list of referees. At the start, you will likely be asking for referral business, but over time—either because you're too busy or the requested work isn't a fit for you—you will want your own list of referee partners to whom you can send potential leads.

   • Make an initial list of potential referees for you.
   • Choose your top three or four and ask for a conversation to learn more.
   • If there is a potential fit, agree (formally by contract or by email) on referral terms. It is important that you have trust with these

partners. You won't be auditing your partners' books. Choose people who can close referred business and who can be trusted to pay you an agreed referral fee.

3. At the start of your business, you will want to use a survey for cold online inquiries to qualify prospects. Later, you may use surveys to decide whether you or someone in your referral network is the best fit for the prospect.

    ◆ Create a survey with five to eight questions that will help you learn from a prospect whether they meet your ICP or are a credible candidate for referral to someone else.

PART 6

SELLING YOU: FROM PROSPECT TO CLOSE

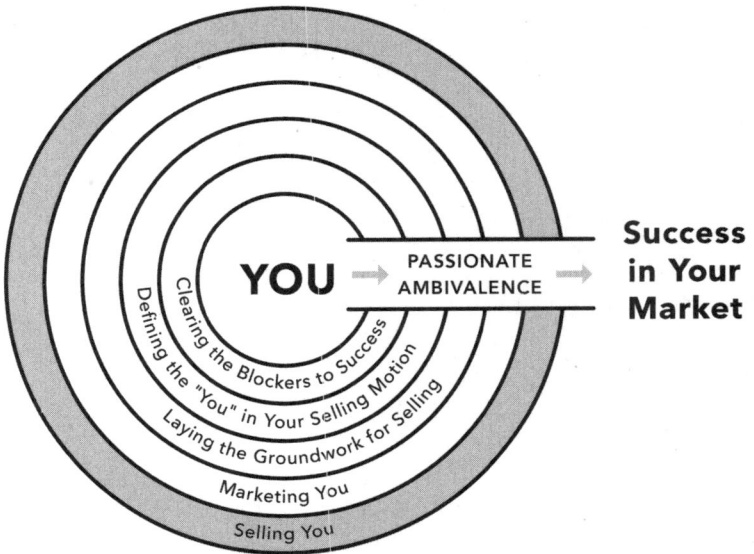

CHAPTER 19

THE UNIFYING THREAD FOR SELLING YOU

Passionate Ambivalence

N ow that your inner work and outer presentation are in great shape, it's time to dig into the mindset and tools of selling. That means it's time for a deep dive into passionate ambivalence.

THE ART OF NOT SELLING

This book is called *Never Ask for the Sale*. As you've seen in the earlier chapters, "never" is a strong suggestion, not a demand. But the point of the title is that not asking for a sale, investment, or job allows you to be an equal in a negotiation. It creates a dynamic where the person evaluating you or what you do senses that getting to work with you is mutually beneficial. That you, especially if you're a solopreneur, are a scarce resource. You are selective. You can create that dynamic successfully through passionate ambivalence, which is the tone, heart, mindset, and philosophy that underlies every sales- and business-building tactic or strategy outlined in this book.

I understand that the phrase "passionate ambivalence" combines two words that appear to be diametrically opposed. But one can be incredibly passionate about something in the present or on the horizon while also being ambivalent about whether it actually happens or whether one is a part of it. I'm not saying that's a simple balance to strike, but I am suggesting that, having done all the work in the earlier chapters, you are ready to strike it.

The single thing that has made me successful in my selling experiences is being secure in myself and my own value. This ensures that I am not desperate to sell anything to anyone, ever. You've seen that I put a ton of work into the steps that precede direct selling. I am dedicated to excellence and learning in all these stages. I do all this advance work so that I can let the system unfold without "needing" any sales outcome to be fulfilled. Of course, there have been times when I believed I needed to make a sale for financial reasons. However, even in those mercifully few moments when I really wanted a sale to close, I have never let myself or my behavior be governed by that mindset. I've never met anyone who wants to be "sold to," and I strongly believe in holding myself and my offerings in a premium position where I am being as selective as my clients. In this way, I rarely come across as needy or sycophantic. I rarely come across as selling in any typical sense.

THE POWER OF PASSION

Let's break down the concept of passionate ambivalence. If I am talking to someone about a potential piece of work, and I am genuinely interested in doing the work, I will openly express my excitement and passion for what the client is looking for, who the client is, and more. Honestly, it's difficult for me *not* to do this. I wear my passion on my sleeves and my pant legs. It's palpable. And I don't really want to hold passion back because I want both my prospect and me to be psyched about the engagement and about doing it together. I want to pause here to note that many of you may be thinking that by expressing passion about a piece of work (or a home during an open house or a new car on a dealer floor), you are compromising your negotiating position. I *strongly* disagree with this view. Instead, I suggest separating your passion about something from your willingness to do it or buy it at any price. Those things are different.

Because I believe that people want to buy from sellers and work with vendors who are passionate about the idea, holding passion back as a means of preserving power is a bad strategy. Very often when a buyer and a seller are fully open to their passion about an activity, a new business process, or a fabulous classic car, the shared excitement might enhance favorable terms for both parties. People (in locations where this practice is still permitted) often write poignant letters to homeowners to accompany an offer for a house in a tough market. They do this because they want the seller to know that this buyer loves the house and has a special connection to it that the seller may value. In many cases, such ovations lead to lower, not higher prices. So be effusive about your authentic passion about the thing. Don't hold back. Instead, showcase ambivalence about price and terms.

THE POWER OF AMBIVALENCE

In the context of selling my solopreneur business, my ambivalence surfaces when talking about whether I will *do* the work with them and the terms under which I'll do it. It starts early in the process, in my first efforts to qualify a prospect when others might simply be willing to take a phone call without any filter. It gets more serious when the negotiation over project scope, price, and terms begins. I also often employ passionate ambivalence in conversations with a prospect about their possible options for getting a piece of work done. If my prospect says something like "Well, Sue, we have found a range of people who are half your price who are great for this engagement," I will generally say, "That's wonderful! You absolutely should hire them!" And they should.

This bifurcation between passion and ambivalence comes up all the time in job negotiations, which is another context where mutual selling happens. One of my clients spoke to me recently about a new role she's considering. The role is perfect for her. It is highly specialized, and she has all the qualifications the role demands. The fact that the hiring company found her is a near miracle because she is as perfect for them as the role is for her. Super. In speaking to my client about how to handle early conversations with the hiring company, I urged her to be open about her passion for the role, but not so open that she would trade on terms that matter a great deal to her to get it. On the content: passion. On the structure and outcome: ambivalence.

Another real-life example of passionate ambivalence came up in my company regarding my calendar availability. I was taking a walk with Leah, and I mentioned that I felt pressure to be available every day of the week, including vacation days. I said, "If I'm not available, people are not going to hire me." Her reply: "Have you ever considered that if you were *less available*, people might *want to hire you more?*" Passionate ambivalence around scheduling has proved to be an excellent approach. Clients work within the contours of my schedule; they frequently comment about how busy I am when they ask me to do something. And I have more time for cycling, front-yard dinner parties, and serving as a groupie for my marathon-running husband. I feel better about my schedule, I feel better about my work, and I feel better about my clients who navigate my calendar because they see the mutual benefit of the engagement.

I engage in ambivalence as a strategy. But for it to work as a strategy, I also need to get myself in position to be unattached to whether I close a deal. This is not an on-off switch. For me, getting to ambivalence is a constant dance. Holding passion while welcoming nonattachment is even trickier.

I have learned that the more passionately ambivalent I am, the more likely I am to meet and beat my goals. In the next chapters, you will read about several ways I engage in passionate ambivalence.

Liz Giorgi, Cofounder and CEO, soona

Before you read further, go find Liz Giorgi anywhere, and everywhere, on social media. Watch her Instagram videos. Read her stories on LinkedIn. And you won't be surprised that, even as Liz's company has scaled, Liz herself reports that she has been responsible for driving 10–15 percent of the company's website traffic.

After that exploration, you also may appreciate that Liz, the cofounder and CEO of soona, is an archetypal example of passionate ambivalence. Just listen to her describe the way she sells: "I'm saying, I understand how you might be feeling, I understand that you might be scared, I understand that you might be struggling to know where you fit, I understand that you might be unsure what the future is. Let me tell you how I think about this right now as a human being with human experiences. Then you can decide if my business is useful to you."

Liz began her career in journalism and launched her first production company, Mighteor, in 2013. Mighteor created ads for the Internet, a nascent business at the time. "I learned that there's so much power in being able to clearly express yourself," says Liz. "If you could clearly express what you were doing and how you and the customer were going to be the best possible superhero pairing, people jumped in.'"

At its peak, Mighteor did $3 million in annual sales. Liz was the only sales-person. "I went anywhere that would have me—events, podcasts, webinars—and talked about the value of video," she says. "I learned to be a great host and story-teller, how to cultivate a relationship with an audience. I never cold-called. I never sent a cold DM. It was always based on me being out in the world telling stories and inviting people to be a part of that story."

By 2019, Liz saw that the merchants she worked with were uniformly frustrated with the process of creating high-quality photos and videos for e-commerce. Liz believed this was a big problem, and one she could solve. She sold Mighteor and used the proceeds to start soona, a virtual production company for e-commerce merchants. She joined the 2019 Techstars Boulder Accelerator, where I was a men-tor. After Techstars, soona raised $1.2 million (some of it from my MergeLane Fund) and took off from there. "We've achieved a level of growth that people just dream of and aspire to," Liz says. "And I feel like a huge part of that has been my success in telling our story and listening to our audience. That approach has never failed me. I've been able to raise capital, close clients, hire great talent, and secure me-dia attention this way. Everything is about creating magnetism. And nothing draws people in like a story.

"There is a kind of a FOMO that a powerful storyteller can generate about get-ting involved in a great business. The sense of excitement, especially at the early stages, makes people want to be a part of the story. So I always try to show people: This is what it could feel like for you to be part of that story. It's a human-focused shared vision, not a transaction."

=====   **EXERCISE**   =====
Your Passionate Ambivalence

When I interviewed Liz for this book, she had a direct message for readers:

> I think a lot of you reading this book are scared of sharing your-
> selves, of being misunderstood, of being seen as boastful or
> false. This isn't about any of those things. It's about just getting
> back to that very truth, which is: We don't want to be sold. At
> all. We want to be understood. We want to be part of a story.

+ Consider Liz's point of view and how it relates to your own experience of selling environments when you have been the customer. This might be listening to a software pitch at work or
  shopping at a clothing store. What behaviors in salespeople
  generate trust for you or increase your interest in a product or
  service? What turns you off? Can you remember a selling experience when the seller was passionately ambivalent—excited
  about what they were selling but unattached to whether you
  made a purchase?
+ Think about three things you've done in past selling that might
  have suggested desperation, neediness, or subservience (the opposite of passionate ambivalence). For example, one of my clients finished a prospect meeting and then "floated a text" once or
  twice a week to a prospect even if the prospect wasn't responding.
+ Think of one of your unique strengths and jot down a talking
  point for discussing that strength using passionate ambivalence.
  For example, "A strength of mine is detail orientation. That's not
  for everyone. For clients who love off-the-cuff meetings and perpet-
  ual brainstorming in lieu of driving to action, I may be a poor fit."

CHAPTER 20

YOU HAVE A PROSPECT!

Now What?

Y ou've done every step of this solopreneur selling journey up to this point, and due to all your diligent, self-reflective, and expressive work, you have a prospect! First, cue the trumpets. Really. It's not simple to go from zero to prospect, and here you are. Great job!

Now what?

QUALIFY YOUR PROSPECT

First, you want a bit more information about your prospect to help you understand how qualified they are. By qualified, I mean how likely they are to be a suitable client or customer paying your target rates. You want to know where they are on their buying journey so that you can initiate a sales effort that meets them and brings them along. Understanding your customer's journey to engaging with you matters immensely. First, it helps you to know how much time you should invest in that prospect. Second, the qualification process is a critical stage for building in passionate ambivalence and increasing the likelihood of selling a meaningful piece of business to a strong prospect at desirable price points.

Here are the common stages of prospect interactions for most solopreneurs (and maybe for most businesses of any size). I list these prospect stages from least qualified to most qualified to purchase a product or service at a satisfactory price for the seller (you). These contact types are ordered from least to most likely to close. This is an imperfect science, and new information can change your point of view, but I'm illustrating these examples in broad strokes so that you can make the best choice on how to handle these incoming leads.

- Random contact email submitted on your site from someone who wants to sell *you* something. These will often be marketing agencies, web developers, copywriters, podcast "agents," pay-for-play media agencies, ghostwriters, accountants, lawyers, or other providers of services for solopreneur-led businesses.
- Random LinkedIn connection request from someone who is trying to sell you something or who wants to expand their network. They want to chat to see how you might be able to support each other.
- Contact from a person or a company that did a Google search for "people who do _____" and arrived at your site. They are asking for a call, proposal, or pricing guidance on how you might support their needs.
- Contact from someone who read an article called the "10 Best People to Work with on _____" and reached out to you because you were on that list.
- Contact from someone who read a blog or listened to a podcast featuring you. They mention why your comments or ideas landed with them, and they want to learn more (and do not seem to be trying to sell you something).
- Contact from a person who heard about your work from a friend or family member of yours and wants to chat with you more about it.
- Contact from a person who worked with you in a prior life or who talked to a person who worked with you in a prior life and who now wants whatever you're selling.

- Contact from a person who heard about your expertise from a person who worked with you in your current capacity as a solopreneur or in a previous chapter as a solopreneur.
- Contact from a person who knows what you do from any of the aforementioned sources and needs that thing done (or started) in the next two weeks.

There are heaps of reasonably priced software tools for small and mid-size businesses that can help you organize a database of leads or prospects. There are low-priced levels of Salesforce, Hubspot CRM, Pipedrive, Streak, and Copper. You can also adapt any task management system to operate as a customer relationship management (CRM) tool using your own system or templates available for tools like Asana, Trello, GQueues, Todoist, and more. Use something that works for you.

MOVE YOUR PROSPECTS THROUGH YOUR FUNNEL

Sales and marketing practitioners use the term "funnel" to describe the path of a prospective customer to becoming an actual customer. At the top of the funnel, you'll find prospects in the early stages. Midfunnel represents prospects who are closer in connection to you or your work but are not ready to buy. Down-funnel or bottom-of-the-funnel prospects are those that are very familiar with or have bought in to you and your work. They're ready to work with you, pending pricing and other logistical and contract elements that might need to be squared away first.

When I think about managing my prospect flow, my goal is to move the prospects who seem like great fits for my business further down in the funnel to get them closer to saying yes. I'm just as interested (if not quite as happy) to move them out of the funnel after getting an efficient no. Even if I don't get that business, I save the time. In considering *how* to move prospects down the funnel, I evaluate these variables:

- How qualified is this prospect? How long or how much work might it take to get them to yes?

- How many people does it seem this prospect is speaking to about the thing I do so I can assess my likelihood of winning this piece of business?
- How much time will it take me to better qualify a prospect (move them from top to midfunnel, for example) given the opportunity cost of that time?
- How likely is this prospect to be able to pay my rates based on some quick research and signals they provide? To evaluate this as well as I can, I review, for example, LinkedIn profiles of the leaders; previous investment history as documented in standard business outlets (if the prospect is a startup), including TechCrunch; and the apparent size of revenues based on case studies and customers shown on the prospect website.
- How likely am I to want to work with this prospect based on some quick research?
- How much time do I have to do *the work* with this prospect on a reasonable timeline given other demands (personal and professional)?

CUSTOMIZE YOUR SALES MOTION

Now that you are armed with these questions, and assuming that you do have other highly leveraged ways to use your time (if it's day one for you, you may consider every prospect worth investigating, so just do that), I would like to suggest how to handle each of the prospect scenarios I listed previously. You'll notice that I strongly warn against treating these different types of prospects in the same way. They are radically different, and your responses should be attuned to where each type of prospect sits in the qualification or funnel scheme.

The Sellers

These are often marketing agencies, web development people or contract companies, copywriters, podcast "agents," pay-to-play media agencies, ghostwriters, accountants, lawyers, or other providers of services to businesses.

Unless I'm extremely interested in what someone in one of these buckets is selling, I completely ignore these contacts. I unsubscribe. On my site contact form, I require submitters to check a box that reads, "I am not trying to sell Sue anything through this form." If I happen to think someone's pitch could help advance my business (or some other goal), I will use a qualification method to ensure that the contact is genuine and especially interested in supporting my goals. A simple reply along these lines can work:

> Hey, I don't usually respond to sales outreach emails, but you are doing something I think could advance my objectives. I imagine you've (or an AI has) written hundreds of these emails today alone. Can you please take a moment and let me know why you think you would be the perfect fit for what I'm up to in the world? I look forward to reviewing your custom and thoughtful response, and we can go from there.

If you do not get the requested custom response, that correspondence is complete.

I don't do this myself, but I know plenty of great people who do outbound email outreach, and I want to ensure that I don't close the door to them entirely when, in your case, they may really fuel your progress.

Random LinkedIn Connection Request

I ignore these touches almost completely except in the rare instance when they are people in my local community or in an underrepresented group that I'd like to support, at least to the extent of making them a first-degree connection.

Because we're on the topic of LinkedIn and prospects, I want to mention that I am very responsive to connection requests, particularly from anyone I've met or anyone who might have a network superior to mine in the area in which I operate. In fact, I religiously reach out to request a connection from anyone who meets these two criteria. I generally do not do outbound marketing after someone accepts a request like this because I don't like when people do it to me. However, I know that the additional network reach that a new, well-placed connection might give me will often serve me.

Contact from a Person or a Company That Did an Internet Search

For example, someone searching online for "people who do _____."

You will know how someone found you only if you ask. On my website contact form, I ask, "How did you hear about Sue?" This is a critical qualification question, and the person who responds to it gets a bit more of my attention. However, they are still at the top of the midfunnel in qualification because they might not be telling the truth, and they might have looked at twenty different sites and sent each business a similar note.

This is an instance where if I am *not* extremely busy with client work, I may nurture this more. I may even respond and take a call just from this first contact. Most often, however, I will not. I will endeavor to qualify the prospect further.

I want to qualify this type of lead further for two reasons. First, I am usually busy with client or other work (or hiking), so there is a genuine opportunity cost to engaging with this type of prospect, particularly with a phone call. Remember that a key aspect of my work is to be paid for phone calls. That time is valuable. If I had a raft of business development representatives on my bench, I would surely respond enthusiastically, because the opportunity cost would be lower for their time than for mine. But I don't. Second, I don't want to immediately agree to a phone call with this type of prospect because it *undermines my likelihood of closing and my price point.*

This is not intuitive. This is passionate ambivalence at work.

You might have read that and thought, *Wait, Sue, if you don't aggressively respond in these situations, you won't get the work, so you'll never even get to a pricing conversation.* I don't disagree, but I respond in a way that enhances rather than undermines my value proposition. I qualify.

In these situations, I write back with something appropriate that makes the prospect do a bit more homework. If they do the mini-assignment, I know they're serious and are more invested in working with me. I will say something like this:

> Thank you so much for finding me on Google and for reaching out about the possibility of working together. I like what you're doing [thing they're doing sourced from my contact form, which requests

their URL and LinkedIn profile link], and this could be a fit. That said, I get a large volume of online inquiries, and I want to protect my time and yours. I'd be grateful if you would look at my site at www.HeySue.com and let me know what about me makes you think I'm a great fit for what you're after. That will advance our conversation. Further, I want to let you know that if you're speaking to more than three people or companies about this opportunity, I'll bow out now. I generally find those large-net searches to be a poor use of time.

You know my style well enough at this point to know what I am up to in this type of reply. Yes, I want to protect my time and not proceed down useless rabbit holes. I'd rather play outside than do a pointless prospect call. But the more important point is that I've injected a *substantial amount of salesmanship* in this email reply. I've shared that I'm busy. I've implied that any decision to work together would be mutual. I've let them know that I am not interested in being a part of major sales beauty pageants, which conveys my sense of my own value. I am *certain* that this type of email reply has resulted in some lost business; however, I'm also certain that any losses are outweighed by what I've gained through this approach in terms of likelihood to close and price premium.

I received an inquiry like this through my site recently, and it is worth reviewing as an example of this category of prospect:

Hello Sue, I hope you're having a great day so far. My name is _____, and I'm a training and development coordinator for _____. We are a full-service digital marketing agency specializing in Affiliate Marketing, Email Marketing, Paid Search & Social, and Creative & Development. We are currently looking into leadership workshops/trainings for our leadership team for the month of July. I came across your content and would like to inquire more about your pricing and availability. Would you be able to provide pricing, availability, and any speaking kits you may have? We can also chat on Zoom/Teams or by phone if you would prefer. Hope to chat with you soon! Best regards, _____

This query wasn't spam because it mentioned my name, referred to the category of work I do, wasn't selling me anything, and shared a deadline for the work just one month in the future. However, given a moderate level of other work, I spent some but not a lot of time on this lead. I replied by thanking the person; sharing a one-page, prewritten PDF about a one-day team workshop with me; and indicating that I would provide pricing and availability in a more advanced discussion. I informed the prospect of my minimum day rate (saving us both time). I said that I do not have a speaking kit, because I don't. I wrote that if everything looked interesting given all that context, I would set up a call with them if they were speaking to no more than two other vendors for this potential work. I think this is a credible response given the attenuated nature of the contact. And it's written, authentically, to reflect boundaries I hold around my time and my work with low attachment to whether I hear back from this person.

I will say this many times in this book. This type of detachment, unavailability, indifference to signing new business quickly—passionate ambivalence—will *increase almost every measurable key performance indicator in selling*. At every stage in the funnel, including pricing and closing, you want to let your prospects know that they are getting something special. This is just the beginning of deploying that strategy in the very first conversation you have with a prospect.

Contact from Someone Who Read an Article

For example, someone reading an article titled the "10 Best People to Work with on _____" and then reaching out to you because you were on the list.

If you land yourself on a "best of" list from a credible source, you will get these types of inquiries. I have had success closing them.

I like these types of prospects, and I pour some qualification energy into them. I wouldn't if I had less time, but it still might be a fine idea. My response goes something like this:

Thank you so much for reading that article on "22 Top Executive Coaches You Can Learn from Today" on CultureAmp.com. I am thrilled to be recognized there, and I'm happy you saw that piece and reached out. As you surely know, my time is my most precious resource. I imagine that's true on your end, too. There were twenty-two amazing people on that list. You may have reached out to all of them! If that's the case, good for you. I prefer not to go deeper (with a phone call) with people doing searches of this scale. However, if you haven't reached out to more than five on this list, I'd love for you to tell me what in that story made you think I would be a great fit for you or your company. You can also look at www.HeySue.com for some additional context on what I'm all about. I look forward to hearing from you and continuing the conversation.

Contact from Someone Who Read a Blog or Listened to a Podcast Featuring You

This is a strong prospect. They already have connected with something you believe, and they likely had to do a bit of legwork to contact you. The only thing I might want to know here before committing to a thirty-minute chemistry or fit call is what kind of project this individual or company is looking to do. They may have said that in their outreach. If they did, and it's something you do and want to do with someone or some company like them, great. If not, get a bit of clarity before offering a call. Once you have that, offer to do a fit call and see what emerges from there. I will cover the initial chemistry call in Chapter 22.

Contact from a Person Who Heard from a Friend or Family Member

This type of prospect is just about as well qualified as the preceding type. I would treat it in the same way. The only difference is to consider who the friend or family member is, how qualified they are to accurately represent what you do, and how well respected they are in the sector you serve. If all those answers are positive, and especially if the family member or friend is meaningful to you, offer a thirty-minute fit call. Also, remember to thank the person who mentioned you in a subsequent email.

Contact from a Person Who Worked with You in a Prior Life

This is a highly qualified person because this prospect knows you not just from a friend or family member at a bar mitzvah but from the work you've done, which may be similar to the work you do now. They either know you and trust you in a work setting or have heard about you from someone who does. Provided this person or company seems to be able to afford your price points (based on your quick research), I would immediately offer a thirty-minute fit call.

Contact from a Person Who Heard About Your Expertise

This includes contact from a person who worked with you. This prospect is more qualified than the preceding person because they either are or know someone who is a current or former client of your solopreneur business. Provided this person or company seems able to afford your price points (based on your quick research), this is an almost certain yes to an introductory call. Again, thank the person who mentioned you to this prospect.

Contact from a Person Who Knows What You Do from Any of the Aforementioned Sources

This person needs something done (or started) in the next two weeks. This prospect has a very high likelihood of closing with far less price sensitivity because of the urgency of their project. Even if this prospect knows you less well or through a less well-connected source (e.g., an article about you), their timeline makes them a hot prospect. Provided this person or company seems like a good fit with the ability to pay for what you do at your price points (based on your quick research), do a high-priority fit call to see if you can meet their immediate needs through a near-term engagement. Obviously, you need to have near-term availability to make this work.

GLOBAL SCENARIOS

These three scenarios apply globally across every prospect scenario:

1. Future referrals. If the prospect is someone or some company that could refer you to high-value business, it almost doesn't matter how they show up in your funnel. Even if *they* are unlikely to be a right customer at the right price point, I will typically speak to them to add them to my flywheel. If we have a great conversation where we determine that we are not a fit for each other, the chances that they will refer me to someone who is a fit in the future are increased by making a high-value connection.

2. No interest? No go. If the prospect is associated with a company or cause you have an aversion to or no interest in, politely decline without spending additional time. If a prospect is asking you to do something that is in your zone of competence or incompetence and you have no desire to get better at that thing as part of your business, politely decline. In some cases, these scenarios may present opportunities for you to refer that prospect to someone in your network.

3. Setting a floor. I don't generally discuss pricing and scope of work with a prospect until after a call. I choose not to do this because I think it undermines my likelihood of closing at a desirable price point. It also may be a waste of time if there is a default in this prospect that I can't uncover until we speak in person. There is only one exception to this rule for me. I am on the high side of pricing in my specializations. As such, it is a qualification tool to mention the floor for pricing for various types of prospects sooner rather than later. This protects my time, as it's generally unproductive to do a dazzling initial chemistry call and find out my prices aren't workable for a prospect. Setting a floor sets expectations, and because strong pricing is a positive differentiator, it helps me position myself as a relevant player in any prospect's consideration set. Finally, establishing

a floor helps me immediately know whether I should route a prospect to a less expensive referral partner.

A FEW FINAL THINGS TO REINFORCE

+ How you handle these prospects sets you up for closing the right prospects at the right price point.
+ Qualifying prospects rather than just opening your schedule to meet with them will increase, not decrease, your likelihood of closing the right prospects at the right price points.
+ Your engagement with prospects who end up becoming clients *starts* with the first inquiry. You are working with them from that moment on. That's the context for anything you say or do as you manage your lead funnel.
+ If you are just getting started, your opportunity cost of any incremental meeting is essentially zero. Talk to almost anyone.

EXERCISE
Establish Your System for Addressing Prospects

+ Evaluate the contact form on your website. Your website should have a contact form. I've recommended a few questions that work for me—company URL, LinkedIn profile link, how you heard about me, verify that you're not trying to sell me anything, and CAPTCHA (for spam mitigation). Check your contact form and make good decisions on how you might like to use it as a tool to optimize the quality of your incoming leads.
+ Set up your canned responses. Use any system you like—Gmail snips, TextExpander, Mac keyboard shortcuts, etc.—to set up canned email responses for any of the prospect personas that are relevant to your marketing and sales funnel. Name each snip in a way that will remind you which persona should get which response. These canned emails are editable for a specific situa-

tion, but it's a great time saver to have them on hand. It will also remind you of where to set boundaries to optimize your time or increase your chances of closing at your desired price points by using qualifying techniques in your contact responses.

- Set up your tracking system. If you haven't already done so, set up a tracking flow for your prospects. Plenty of tools integrate with Google Workspace or Microsoft Teams to automate this. Be sure to track the date of initial contact, type of lead (based on a set of definitions you craft, perhaps informed by those previously listed), your response (date and content), next steps, likelihood to close percentage, and the likely dollar value of the engagement. Those are basic, and they should serve most solopreneur businesses well. You can always add or subtract fields as you learn how to gain even more visibility in this part of your sales process.

CHAPTER 21

THE POWER OF SAYING NO

S aying "no" in a selling context warrants its own chapter because many of you (especially the newbies) will regard the idea of declining business as between contrarian and insane. Our culture promotes the idea that a sale is a win. The customer (or prospect) is always right. I see you. I have been tempted at times to be you. I empathize with you if your bank balance is low this month and it's time to pay rent. Furthermore, I give you a complete permission slip to take nonaligned paying business when you need to.

However, I believe it is imperative for you to begin to appreciate the power of saying no in building the business or selling effort you admire: one that will ultimately deliver to you the rich rewards of working on enlivening work with clients you love at rates that are optimal for you. So even if this chapter feels a bit aspirational, even if it is more of an opening to say maybe than no, follow along, stay with the mindset it outlines, and keep it, at a minimum, in the back of your mind for the times when it may come in handy.

During every stage of the prospecting and selling process, I remain constantly aware of the option of politely declining a piece of work. This is perhaps the most concrete outgrowth of passionate ambivalence I can imagine.

RED FLAGS

As I learn about a prospect and an opportunity, I occasionally uncover red flags. Sometimes they are about the prospect or about the setup of the work itself. Sometimes the flags concern my sense of what I want to do at a given time. Sometimes the flags relate to fit. Other times, the flags arise in the context of negotiating price or the terms of an agreement. In every instance, I endeavor to see the flags and, at a minimum, discuss my concerns with the prospect. If I don't receive a satisfying response, I politely decline the work.

If I have a poor fit with a person, company, or scope of work, I will fail in my own mind. Failure includes both doing a poor job and being unhappy and unfulfilled. Those things go together, of course.

YOUR WILLINGNESS TO SAY NO, POSSIBLY TWICE

Everything you'll read for the rest of this book will be based on the assumption that you are a passionate, ambivalent solopreneur who is willing to say no. I have said no *after embarking* upon a long-term engagement. I've had a feeling that something is off. I have had a conflict of values. I have had a sense that I'm not doing enough to benefit a client. In some of those situations, I have contacted the client, articulated my belief that I sensed misalignment, and returned all unused funds. Again, it is never fun to write big checks that immediately knock down profits. But in each case, I've felt lighter and happier, and the space occupied by the inappropriate work has been filled with something far more satisfying.

I have one quick warning: Because passionate ambivalence is such a powerful sales tool—as well as a healthy context from which to embark on a sales process and build your business—you may try to politely decline a piece of work and find that your prospect wants you even more. You know the situation of a company that unwisely waits too long to promote an employee and then jumps through hoops to retain the employee after she gets a great offer somewhere else. People often gravitate to unavailable people. Watch for a big reaction to a polite declination.

I am *not* recommending politely declining work as a *tool* to increase your prospect's appetite or raise your price point. I think that's dishonest. But I do want you to be aware that if you do decline, you may receive a very forceful response. So be clear on your declinations, and, absent some material change in the facts after an authentic conversation, adhere to them.

CHAPTER 22

HOW TO CONDUCT A "FIT CALL"

have not titled this chapter "How to Make a Pitch." Why? Passionate ambivalence. Deciding to make a sale and commit to a project is a mutual decision. That's a critical element of deploying passionate ambivalence at this stage of the sales process.

Let's say you have a qualified prospect that you want to work with. You have agreed that you and the prospect will do what I call a "chemistry" or "fit" call to see if your skills, pricing, and approach are a good match. Fit calls are mutual vetting exercises.

My fit calls are always thirty minutes long. I love these calls. When I see them on my calendar, I get excited. I have already passed through a series of qualification gates to get to this point, as you've read. I've already decided I likely want this work. This is not a first date—this is a first weekend road trip with someone you think you might really like.

My goals for a fit call are to

+ Make a genuine connection.
+ Learn about the prospect.
+ Let the prospect get an authentic sense of my style and my two-minute bio.
+ Get a feel for their needs in wanting to work with me, both explicit and implicit.

- Be in a position to say no. That means pitching well enough to get the engagement, knowing that if I decide later that something didn't feel right, I can politely decline.
- Feel that I have given the prospect the experience of working *with me* on the call.
- Contribute one insight of value to the prospect, regardless of whether we ever speak again.
- Have fun!

To achieve these goals, I show up for fit calls with all the energy, challenge, love, and humor I can muster. I am relaxed. I am happy (I might have mentioned that I love selling). I am fully present, in the moment, on my edge, prepared for any development that might require my full attention and nimble reaction. I am putting my best foot forward to be interesting and likable and to evaluate the same qualities in the prospect. I want to see if I feel a sense of kinship with the prospect.

When I do a fit call, I *absolutely do not sound like I am selling*. Active, pointed, typical "selling" is the antithesis of authentic connection and passionate ambivalence. I certainly can't effectively sell without first achieving some level of relationship. And I want to tell you what I mean when I say that and how I do it.

FIT CALL PREP

To prepare for a fit call, I spend about fifteen minutes learning what I can about the prospect. As I mentioned earlier, by this point, I have decided I likely want this work. However, I don't overinvest or get too attached to the idea of actually working with this person or company because I want to stay unattached in our discussions about whether I still want to work with them based on what unfolds in the call. In addition, the prospect may opt out of working with me during or after the call, so I try to keep my mind open and balanced to stay in a state of passionate ambivalence. By the time of the call, I have quickly read everyone's LinkedIn profiles. I like knowing the threads that connect career stories. I also like knowing where in a person's past we have some overlap in background, as that is often fodder for connection. I have also reviewed the website of the prospect's organization to get a sense of culture and focus. If I've asked the prospect qualifying questions, I've reread their responses.

I'm ready.

I do almost all fit calls over video because I think I am more compelling with voice and video than with voice only. It also helps me to pick up on visual cues that can be helpful in making the kind of connection that drives a successful close. I almost never do important fit calls at airports or other places where there is a high risk of tech disruption or distractions. I want to be completely present. That said, I do not dress up for these calls. I show up as me, usually quite casual, which for me means one or two steps up from just having returned from the gym. I want to be authentic on these calls, so there's no blazer on top and gym shorts on the bottom happening over Zoom for me. This is all intentional. Casual is one of my core brand attributes, and I want to convey it accurately from the start.

THE ART OF ASKING QUESTIONS

I spend the first twenty minutes of most calls running the meeting. I ask questions, and I listen very carefully to the answers so that my follow-up questions will be relevant and smart. In my experience, the quality of your questions and your listening are two critical determinants of your sales success.

Two formative experiences contributed to my development as an asker of good questions. First, my dear grandmother Elisa helped me understand that the way to make friends and be loved in life is to be someone who asks excellent questions and pays attention to the answers. She taught me when I was very young that people love to talk about themselves. It makes them feel special.

I ripened my talent for asking excellent questions as a trial lawyer. As a federal prosecutor in financial crimes and civil rights cases, I found that there was nothing better than getting a shot at cross-examining the defendant. I noticed that some trial lawyers crafted detailed scripts for the questions they planned to pose on cross-examination. I couldn't believe that. Why on earth would I craft a highly refined script for an occasion that would almost surely present unexpected opportunities? Sure, I would have a one-page outline of things I wanted to cover or evidence I wanted to authenticate and enter into the record. But I kept my mind open and elastic during cross-examination so that when, inevitably, the defendant or another important defense witness revealed something surprising, I could seize that opportunity. Because of my grandmother's great training and the added benefit of having been raised by a pack of lawyers, I could be nimble and improvisational when questioning witnesses. That skill paid dividends and still does.

For me, asking great questions is part nature, part nurture. It just happens to be an excellent strategy for selling (and for executive coaching and facilitation), and it shines most brightly during chemistry calls with prospects.

GREAT QUESTIONS REFLECT AND CREATE CONNECTION

To make a genuine connection, I pay attention to gaps in what someone is sharing or to opportunities to learn more about a prospect telling me a story. If I'm truly listening, certain questions arise naturally in my mind, and I choose to ask them even if there's a risk of taking someone away from their story arc. I want them to know I'm paying attention and want to understand them better. Here are a few examples of what I consider to be a "good" question:

- A prospect says, "You know, almost anyone would handle this kind of situation this way." You ask, "I hear your story that this is a near-universal response, but I'm curious why *you* chose to react that way? What in your background or belief system led to that outcome?"
- A prospect says, in a louder or faster vocal range, "It really didn't matter; that wasn't what was important." If you notice that sounds fishy, you might ask, "Are you sure that didn't matter? Can you help me understand why that's irrelevant since you mentioned it?"

+ A prospect says, "I got this feedback on my annual review. I'm annoyed by it because I thought I was doing better at that over the last year." You ask, "What about that feedback specifically is hard for you to hear? Is it familiar in situations beyond just your last annual review?"

THE SCOPE OF THE CALL

During the first twenty minutes, when I'm taking the lead, I'm working to create impressions about myself while learning more about my prospect and the services they need. After that block of time, I open things up by saying something like "What would you like to know about me?"

During the last ten minutes, I almost certainly find a way to share my two-minute bio. I believe my background makes me perfectly suited to do the work that I do, and I want my prospect to know that. However, *I never say anything close to those words.* Why? Because I want to practice passionate ambivalence. Instead, I subtly tweak my background to showcase facts or stories that I think might be relevant to this prospect and the work they need. They've likely never read my two-minute bio (unless, like you, they're reading this book!).

Often, during the last part of a fit call, a prospect will ask me a question that is either unanswerable or answerable only in a way that requires me to oversell. In my work, the most common such question is "How can we know that we'll get solid results from working with you?" If I were an accountant, I might be able to answer this question in a concrete, low-emotion way. But I'm not an accountant, and most often I can't give an affirmative response that is objective. Many of you reading this book may not have a clear answer, either.

When a question like this is asked and I'm at my best, I most often respond in a way that seems to be selling against myself. I do this to achieve three things:

1. Show passionate ambivalence.
2. Be absolutely clear about what I don't do.

3. Send a very confident and very authentic disconfirming sales message about what *I am fairly sure I will accomplish.*

This maneuver is subtle, but I want to cover everything from the basics to the ninja moves. So here you go. The conversation might go something like this:

Prospect: What provable results or impact do you believe you'll have if we spend an off-site day working with you?

Sue: (point 1, showing passionate ambivalence) Thanks for asking. It makes sense for you to ask. However, we haven't done the day yet, so I can't really tell you this. What I can tell you is that I have a set of tools I use. At worst, your team will walk away with a shared set of approaches and a shared vocabulary for how to work better together on that specific issue you just said you wanted to improve.

Prospect: How can I justify this significant expense without a clear sense of the outcomes?

Sue: (point 2, absolute clarity about what I don't do) Look, I think there are several coaches and facilitators who work with very complex metrics-based approaches to engagements like this. For me, this is taking highly subjective data and making it seem objective. I don't do that. I'm not interested in it, and I don't think it's best for teams like yours. The reason is that you want a facilitator who comes with a plan that is flexible so she can respond to whatever shows up in the room on that day with your team. That is what I'm great at, and that is why you heard about how much value I added to your friend's last executive off-site.

Prospect: I hear you, and my friend said you were amazing, but it's a valuable day, not just your fee but also the cost of the time of my executive team.

Sue: (point 3, confidently and authentically delivering a disconfirming sales message about what *I am fairly sure I will accomplish*) You are absolutely right about that, and I do not take that lightly. It is a straight-up privilege to do what I do with people like you and your team. It sounds crazy to tell you this because it is not provable, but my goal for every session is to rapidly create a climate where you and your team can address underlying, recycling issues in a matter of hours that will otherwise cost you months or years in productivity. My goal isn't just to have a great, productive day with you. It is to create a spirit of complete, positive transformation for your team. If that doesn't happen, I'll be disappointed. That may sound like a specious claim, but the reason I do this and not something else is because, more often than not, that happens. And when it does, it's a big win for us all.

EMBRACE THE LIMITS AND SET BOUNDARIES

I want to reinforce that this is not a parlor trick. I believe everything I said in this hypothetical chat. In this example, I am doing an important thing: I am not giving the prospect what they think they want. The reason is that I cannot genuinely do that. If I tried to give them what they say they want, I would be in a position of overselling (or essentially lying) to tell them what they want to hear. I am saying no. There are limits. I can't tell you 100 percent that you will get outcome X. I can tell you that I can do actions Y and Z and that they often produce X. But no, I can't promise you X. This setting of boundaries is a selling technique that calls up passionate ambivalence. But more than that, it's genuine. It's a way for me to stay in integrity. The reason integrity works for me as a sales tool is that authenticity is one of my core values. It's a brand attribute. Typically, when my ICP hears this from me, they are more rather than less likely to choose me.

I have had conversations like this hypothetical chat many, many times, perhaps in 50 percent of my fit calls. In these situations, I am *authentically* selling beliefs I hold, hopes I have, using a tenor that is exactly what you would find if we met over coffee. At every stage, I am being myself and giving my prospect a chance to know who I am so that they can vet our fit as well. I am being extremely passionate about my work and often about my prospect, because at this stage, I generally am. You have a version of this for you. Consider how you might pull through the threads I'm sharing in a language that feels and is authentic to you.

Can you see how selling against myself in points one and two opens the door for me to get a bit cocky in point three? Of course it doesn't work every time, but generally, if a client is a great fit, this positioning is so authentic to me and so desirable to them that they'll take a risk with me. (I have a 100 percent money-back guarantee, which helps as well. I may bring that up in a fit call, but it's been used only once in ten years for a $400 refund, so most often I don't. I'll share more on the psychology of that guarantee in the pricing chapter.)

In these thirty-minute calls, by guiding the conversation through deeper and more informative questions—including asking the prospect for their questions—I am endeavoring to give the prospect a chance to notice things about me that I believe make me very good at my job.

I am also evaluating whether I want to take on a particular piece of work with this person or company. That's why passionate ambivalence is honest. To make that point obvious, I occasionally mention what is also true: I am busy; I have plenty of work; I have the privilege of being selective about the work that I do. I convey these messages subtly because if I'm not subtle, I am missing that brilliant tone of ambivalence.

BUILDING RELIABLE TRUST: HONESTY AND VULNERABILITY

I'm digging in deep, establishing that I can quickly create a setting where people can speak candidly and vulnerably about important issues. Sometimes this depth surfaces important themes I want to face with my prospect if we work together. In a recent fit call with a senior leader, my prospect made several allusions to his static marriage. He said the marriage was "fine," that coaching would be about work and not therapy, and that we didn't need to focus on the personal. It became apparent to me that a pattern of accepting mediocrity cut across his life. It was unlikely that we could have a valuable 1:1 coaching relationship if work and his personal dynamics were not on the table.

I said that I didn't want to coach him if his personal life was off-limits. I look for common threads across my clients' lives to spark insights from one area that might be useful in others. I also shared that working with me might create some discomfort for him if he's committed—consciously or unconsciously—to being unhappy and unsatisfied.

I'm the type of coach who pushes edges, and he should work with me only if he thinks that loving push might be what he's after—even if he wouldn't have said that before our call. Although I was giving him reasons to *object* to working with me, I also built a great deal of trust in that dialogue. It's no fun for either of us if our styles don't sync. He became a client, but it would have been fine either way.

In a typical fit call, I'm establishing my intellect by making connections among the themes my prospect raises, and I'm also asking questions that reflect the advance research I've done. I want my prospects to sense that I'm a quick study. They won't need to spend hours or days bringing me up to speed. I am often up to speed when I start, thanks to calls like this.

I'm generally using the questions I ask and the way I respond to the answers to create what I hope is an accurate impression that I am trustworthy. Nothing I say in a first or last call is useful if the person on the other end of the Zoom call doesn't feel they can believe me.

To establish authenticity, I am as direct as I usually am, and I often find a way to say something vulnerable or revealing about myself. The decision to share something about myself is not a hippie, kumbaya move. I've learned that the flip side to being a great questioner is that others occasionally feel that talking with me is a one-way street. I may elicit a ton of information from them and share nothing of myself. I've received feedback—most often offered in friendship and not sales contexts—that this feels uneven and inhibits others' trust in me. So I've taken this feedback and applied it to selling.

Revealing the true me is not a sales tool except that it is a deep part of how I build reliable trust with people. It's a behavior that is true to me in every context of my life. It's easy. And it's real.

In fit conversations, I want to ensure that my prospect knows I'm superb. I want them to know that I'm busy, respected, well-connected, deeply passionate about my work, and able to do things that are valuable enough to my clients that I'm worth hiring at a premium price.

I also reveal characteristics of myself that are unique, including those that are less than stellar. I want prospects to know I'm special, and I want to be honest in presenting myself to ensure that we are having an honest call to assess fit. *I routinely share reasons I think we may not be a good fit.* Again, this serves two purposes: It helps me be honest, and it often helps me establish myself as more desirable in the eyes of my prospects. This is the work of passionate ambivalence.

The central feature I reveal about myself is that I am a loving challenger. I am not a person who coddles. I am a person who pushes. I am oriented toward increasing depth, welcoming tension in service of greater candor, and helping my clients (individuals and groups) unlock the highest version of their potential. For me, this doesn't come through passive caretaking. It comes from a willingness to take risks and speak my version of truth to power. When I mention this, I often say something like "I imagine you have picked up on this feature of me in this call. I hope you have." I also often say, "If this tone isn't quite right for you or the project you're working on, I may not be a fit."

Why do I say that last thing? First, because it's true. Second, if I have a hunch that I am a *great fit* for the engagement, it's an excellent use of passionate ambivalence.

ENDING THE CALL AND NEXT STEPS

I want to end every fit call with a concrete next step. Sometimes that next step is a piece of work that we've agreed to in that same call. Approximately 40 percent of my first calls end with an agreement to get to work. If a call doesn't end in a green light or a red light (which may come from either of us), I want one next step. I might ask my prospect to "sit with this and let me know what you think when you form a clear thought." That kind of ending happens often in a fit call when I am one of two or three people to whom a prospect is speaking. It is also a superb example of passionate ambivalence because I am intentionally *not* requesting a decision right at that moment. The other likely next step is for me to deliver something to the prospect, often a summary scope of work and pricing. Those two major elements of a sale frequently come up during a fit call or in the email follow-up. Those are our next topics. Obviously, if you make a clear commitment to do something at the end of a fit call, you need to do it on the schedule you promised.

===== **EXERCISE** =====
Your Fit Call Template

What are a few aspects of you that you hope come through in a quality fit call?

- For each of those aspects of you, what is one way you could talk about that feature or one example you can give to support that feature in a fit call?
- What are three questions you routinely want to ask a prospect, knowing that you'll flex your script frequently?

CHAPTER 23

PRICING, SCOPE OF WORK, AND BILLING

It's time to talk about pricing, and pricing is polarizing. It should be. Much ink has been spilled on pricing strategy, and you will settle on yours and hopefully revisit it often. Like all the chapters in this part of the book, pricing is a meaningful place to deploy passionate ambivalence. You should have worked out the parameters of your pricing model and have a few ideas about how you might scope an engagement before your first fit calls.

In most businesses that require you to sell yourself to generate revenue, the only real rule of pricing is that you're charging some amount of money for your time or your work that feels good to you at a given stage in your business. In addition, your pricing will contribute to your success in achieving the goals that you laid out in Chapter 12.

My number-one belief about pricing is that it is fluid. My pricing started as a $95 cup of coffee. I had no revenue at all! I just thought there were fifteen people a week asking to have coffee with me. Perhaps two of those would pay me. Then I'd have $190 a week, and I would have established that having coffee with me had some monetary value. That was a win.

Over time, I have increased my prices based on a general sense of the market's tolerance and my sense of how much value I'm conferring on a given piece of work. I've said that I do not do much market research generally, but I collect meaningful data all the time through the normal course of business. I imagine you do, too. For example, occasionally a prospect will push back on pricing, and they will report that the other people they spoke with for the engagement were charging a fraction of my quote. That's useful information, even if it doesn't prompt me to change my price. You also may get the opposite type of data, which is a prospect saying yes to your price immediately. You might wonder whether that quick yes means you were priced below what the prospect expected.

At this point, I do not spend any time interviewing people who do what I do about their price points or researching competitors' websites to get a feel for the market. That said, I have been doing this for so long that I have a good sense of the landscape and what works for me. If you are earlier in your selling efforts, doing a bit of that research, including talking to willing people in your line of work, researching competition, and reading articles about expected rates for what you do will be useful. Over time, the market will ultimately give you most of the answers you need.

FACTORS THAT CONTRIBUTE TO PRICING

Factors largely about me, the seller and provider:

+ How much time will this take?
+ How can I set a price that reflects the value I've built up in myself as a professional and a resource over the last thirty years, the last ten of which were tied to being an executive coach and facilitator?
+ How excited am I to do this?
+ How much will this engagement feel like "work"?
+ How much will I learn and grow in my field?
+ How close is this scope of work to my zone of genius?
+ How busy am I right now or during the time when I would be doing this work?
+ If this request is urgent, how hard will it be to move other pieces of work to accommodate it?
+ What is the opportunity cost (in my professional and personal life) of doing this work?
+ How much revenue do I need to achieve my goal for this period?
+ How likely am I to be successful in this engagement?

+ Will doing this work lead to other work that is at least as good, based on future word-of-mouth referrals?
+ If this work was referred by another professional, how important is it that I honor that referral by doing this work?

Factors largely about the prospect:

+ Can this prospect afford my current minimum rates (my floor)?
+ Can this prospect afford a premium on my floor rates?
+ How time-sensitive is this project for my prospect?
+ How focused is my prospect on working with me, specifically?

I consider all these factors in setting prices. I almost never depart from my current floor rate. If I do, it is because I'm doing something for a very close friend or family member or because the work is related to a social cause that is so compelling that I want to do the work for free or at a steep discount. So usually my options are the floor rate, a premium on the floor rate, a steep discount, or free.

DETERMINING A PRICE OR RATE FLOOR

In determining my floor rate as an executive coach and consultant, I often think about revenue per hour. I *never bill by the hour* because I don't think massive value can be accurately priced this way, but I do think about how many hours it would take me to complete an engagement and what my effective hourly rate would be. That effective but unspoken hourly rate has increased, driving an increase in my floor rate for any engagement.

I have never had a huge problem articulating a healthy floor rate. As I mentioned, I had strong role models in my field who helped me appreciate the value this type of work can generate for clients. In addition, I had healthy goals for my solopreneur business given my previous work as an operations executive. My mortgage and lifestyle were at a certain level, and if I couldn't generate enough revenue through my business, I would need to get another executive job. All this drove my pricing for the first two or three years. Then my goals and my BHAG took over.

I often hear solopreneurs say they struggle to price themselves adequately. I got help early on from Jim Dethmer, who talked about the notions of value and price separately. He encouraged me to consider what the value of my work might be to a given client in a given scope of work. That was X. I could tell my prospect I felt that the value was X, and then I could set a price of Y, which might be lower than X. This framework was useful in managing my imposter voice and pushing forward with pricing that met my goals, even if some prospects declined to work with me because of price.

DENIM: A FORMATIVE STORY ABOUT PREMIUM PRICING

Some of you may be old enough to remember how much a pair of jeans cost in the early 2000s. Nice jeans were about $45. Jeans were available at the Gap, Banana Republic, or a department store. They could be fashionable and cut in specialized ways (heck, I'm old enough to remember those sexy Sasson jeans from the 1970s), but jeans themselves were not generally regarded as a premium luxury item.

All of that changed, and I pin the change to the year 2006 and the brand 7 For All Mankind. I became aware of the change only then. I came to understand that most of the twenty-somethings in my office were wearing $175 jeans. I could not believe this. At the time, it was an exorbitant amount of money for any garment, but jeans? Naturally, I did what any engaged learner would do and surveyed every person in the office, asking them how many pairs of jeans they owned that cost more than $150. The office average was two pairs.

The ridiculous thing that happened next taught me more about pricing than anything else in my life. I went to a fancy "denim store" (because apparently that was now a thing), and *I bought a pair of $175 jeans!* Why? Because I determined that if people were willing to spend that kind of money on a pair of jeans, those jeans *must* be superior. I fell victim to the prestige bias, thinking that the premium price implied a superior brand, better quality, and a finer fit.

This expensive lesson led to two valuable outcomes. First, I really did look better in that $175 pair of jeans. I'm sure of it. Second, I learned about the value of using premium pricing to drive brand and quality perceptions. Although I always believe that my prices are logical and consistent with the value I create for customers, I have never, not for one day, believed that lowering my prices would produce more sales or more overall revenue. I've believed the opposite. This pricing belief fuels passionate ambivalence.

YES, QUALITY OVER QUANTITY

Due to that mentality, I have known that I would not be focused on the quantity of engagements I did in a year. I would optimize for the quality of the engagements and my total revenue or revenue per engagement. That decision has made me more likely to hit my goals, which include both revenue and performance measures, and the looser measure of how much hiking I get to do.

This is my context for thinking about pricing. You get to formulate yours. I simply want to stand for the point of view that lower pricing may counterintuitively lead you to close fewer deals. I also want to be clear that almost everything I have said thus far about pricing incorporates an element of passionate ambivalence: wanting great work but being willing to price at a level some people will not accept, then trusting that in the end, pricing in a way that meets my criteria will lead to better overall revenue performance and a better quality of work and life.

ADDITIONAL PRICING TIPS AND STRATEGIES

There are a few additional beliefs that contribute to how I price my work. I want to let you in on them in case they may serve you and your pricing strategy:

- **Price Your Work Holistically and Not in Component Parts:** You may earn more per unit of time or effort by aggregating your work into a holistic scope of work instead of breaking down your engagement into its component parts. My favorite example is my friend Ashley Darling, a yoga and mindfulness guru who also co-owns a Sonoma winery called Darling Wines. Ashley recounted a story of a San Francisco tech company that contacted her to lead a two-day mindfulness and team-building workshop for its executive team. Ashley told me how she priced the gig: "I told them it would be this much per person for yoga, this much per person for meditation sessions, and this much per person for wine tasting." She told me this story on Zoom, and she started laughing when I raised my palm to my forehead. She'll never do this again, and I don't want you to do it, either.

The value of the whole often is greater than the sum of the parts, and it should be. Finding someone who can teach yoga, run meditation sessions, provide a stunning venue, and conduct brilliant wine tastings with food pairings is *not easy*. Treat your engagement as a whole—conveying the scope of the work and its broadest available effects—versus an aggregation of small parts. If people ask you to break things down, and they may, you can opt out or break things down at a holistic value number. If they challenge your price per one element of the experience, price those components at numbers far higher than a single-feature provider might price them, and stand by it. Alternatively, consider a polite refusal.

◆ **Beware of Efforts to Drive Down Your Pricing Floor by Tweaking Scope:** Your general approach to an engagement likely goes hand in hand with your pricing parameters. That is true for me. For example, I have a belief that a 1:1 coaching engagement should be about six to eight months long. There's nothing sacred about this belief, but it feels like a reasonable amount of time to build a relationship, identify goals, and achieve a positive impact in partnership with a coaching client. I have a pricing floor for coaching engagements and a scope that includes a few details and a bit of structure around a six-to-eight-month plan. At times, prospects have wanted to pay less for a coaching engagement, and the way they sought to do that was to reduce the scope of work, to create a shorter coaching engagement. I have generally politely declined in these situations. That's in part because I very rarely negotiate down from my pricing floor and in part because I believe in the engagement structure I've developed over time.

Somehow, chipping away at a month here or there in my structure feels like nickel-and-diming. I generally dislike that. Allowing it contravenes passionate ambivalence in my view. I don't do it as a buyer, either. I don't ask for discounts on Airbnbs, and I give people raises when I see that their work for me is worth more than I'm paying. I believe in win-for-all pricing. So if someone is attempting to adjust my offering to get to a lower price, I will usually say no. In very rare instances when I think I can do some good work 1:1 with a person in a day or a half day, I will offer a lower price point for a wholly different kind of engagement.

I'm not suggesting that you never be flexible; I'm suggesting that you create a scope of work that makes sense for the outcomes you want, price it accordingly, and endeavor to stay aligned with both your structure and your price point for that structure.

+ **Rarely Bill by the Hour:** Unless you have no other choice, try to stay out of the hourly billing game. Early on, you may have less choice, but try to escape this construct. Why? Because billing by the hour is no fun. Do you really want to clock phone calls? I have been a law-firm lawyer. No one does.

The other reason to steer clear of hourly billing is that it's the epitome of pricing by the unit instead of by the whole. Furthermore, billing by the hour is not great for you if you have a wealth of experience that comes through at the beginning of your engagement. Yes, you can cure some of the first-hours problems by having a very high hourly rate, but most prospects will reject a rate that accurately reflects the value of your first few hours, so you miss out on the premium that your considerable experience deserves.

+ **Charge for Availability Using Minimal Commitments:** Along similar lines, I often see contractors billing by the hour but working whenever their clients decide to engage them on specific tasks.

This is a lousy arrangement for the contractor. The contractor is often expected to be available almost all the time. If the actual work is four hours a week but the client has a "right" to ask the contractor to work on demand, the customer is underpaying the contractor because they are not paying for the contractor's availability during non-hands-on-job time. This is, again, one more reason not to bill by the hour. This scenario can be cured by building in a mandatory minimum monthly retainer. That way, whether the contracting company uses you or not, they are paying for you to hold literal or figurative space (in your days and your brain) to do their work when they need you.

- **If Your Pricing Is Premium, Start with a Shin-in-the-Water Engagement:** I have been able to grow my work with clients over time. It's the best evidence that I am adding value, and they get to expand their use of me based on their needs and timing. I have never pushed for long-term contracts early on to increase my revenue. I often start with a single small engagement so that we can mutually decide whether there is a fit. In fact, the most common scenario in which I engage in a long-term annual contract is when I'm *reducing my effective rates*. If a client has experienced a taste of working with me and they want to bring me in as a company coach with a long-term commitment, I reduce my standard prices in exchange for their commitment. Taking the approach of starting small helps me feel fine about charging premium pricing. It also helps me show up authentically as passionately ambivalent. I'm not pushing them for a long-term yes; I'm simply suggesting that we try this one thing, and if it works, we'll do more together. That has been a very successful strategy for me.
- **Rarely Ask Someone What Their Budget Is:** I will try to avoid an all-out rant here, but with due respect, I think asking a prospect about their budget is the dopiest sales question. The reason is that their budget and your value proposition are different matters altogether. In general, I recommend that you not make their budget your constraint. A budget constraint might mean you don't work with a prospect, but it ought not to alter your pricing. I say this because I

think it makes you look more sophisticated as a seller and because I think this attitude will enhance your likelihood of closing at a desired price. This is another example of passionate ambivalence.

Let me give you an example. Years ago, I was accompanying my friend Kim on her mission to buy a car. We kept walking into dealerships, and within the first few questions, a salesperson would ask Kim what her budget was. Worse, they would ask what she could afford to pay monthly. What? It's not that the question has *nothing to do with* the car Kim might ultimately choose; it's just not a highly relevant question.

The most sophisticated question is about the value of a particular car. From that information, it is Kim's decision whether to purchase that car, either for reasons associated with affordability or for other reasons, like a belief that a specific car wasn't worth that much money to her in relation to other available options.

You're in a dance on pricing. I realize that. But let your prospect push back on budget and give them the impression (preferably an accurate one) that you know the value of your services. Asking about budget undermines your confidence in your pricing structure. If a prospect can't afford your price, you'll sort that out in your fit conversation, but let it emerge naturally rather than making your pricing contingent on their stated (possibly accurate and possibly not) budget.

♦ **Rarely Reduce Your Price in Negotiations:** This rule may not be for you, and it may not apply if you're starting out and not finding enough work to fill your schedule or meet your goals. That said, I personally think I have closed more work at my desired price point by not negotiating on price than I have by negotiating.

When there has appeared to be a price incompatibility, I have often suggested that we are not a fit, and I have often proposed referring a prospect to a colleague who charges less. In *many* instances, those mere suggestions eliminated the pricing gap that existed three minutes earlier. My belief on this point is another example of passionate ambivalence. I believe my aversion to negotiating price down comes into play most often at the beginning of a prospect conversation. Early on, the person you're most often negotiating against is yourself when you start flexing on price. I had a recent example of this when I quoted my price for a scope of work as $20,000, and the CEO, who had extreme time sensitivity for the work, asked me to come down to $18,000. Here was my emailed response to his 10 percent discount proposal:

So. Fees.

I had a negative reaction to your negotiation of fees. I can see that by making myself available as I have for a friend of Chris's might make it seem like I'm largely available. I'm rarely available. Chris is a priority, and I happen to like situations like this.

However, I'm changing things in my universe to do something that I think is urgent. And I'm either incredibly gifted and accommodating you or I'm average or worse. If I'm gifted, and I help you save your team, your budget or my value to the company is well over $20,000. If I'm average, I'm worth nothing. I can't see the difference between $15,000, $20,000, and $25,000 from your vantage point except as a predilection for negotiating, which isn't something I need to or want to indulge. I charged you my normal rates and didn't increase anything for the time sensitivity.

I don't know if I can help. I do know I already want to.

My rates are what they are. I'm sure you can find someone less expensive and good, and if you choose that path, I completely understand.

If you'd like to do this, I'm ready to start on Monday and will send you what you need to get your team rolling.

- **We Agreed to Work Together That Day:** Now, if you get quite far along in a conversation and the prospect and the work feel like a great fit, then just before the finish line, you may make a small price concession to get the deal done. This has happened to me in instances where someone has a grant for coaching or other training. The grant is for $X, and the scope they are asking about costs $X + .1X$. In that situation, all things being green, I probably will let go of the incremental 10 percent.

+ **Have a Very Generous Money-Back Guarantee:** This may not work for you, but if you're superb, it should. It just feels scary the first time you say it. One way I navigate small pricing gaps in prospect conversations is to mention that I have a 100 percent money-back guarantee. It's no joke. I do, and I have from the very beginning of running my me-focused company.

Now, I don't imagine that people can do eight or ten coaching sessions with me and then request their money back for the work we've done in the first eight sessions. But if I'm doing a day with a client and the day goes poorly, or if I do a meeting or two in a six-month engagement and those meetings don't go well, I want to return the engagement fee. I want my work and my pricing to be win-for-all, and that means I need to deliver. I have had one person request a refund for a two-day Leadership Camp. I have returned funds to two clients when I felt I wasn't being of tremendous service. That's the extent of uses of my guarantee over ten years, but I continue to offer it because I think it's a security rail for prospects whom I'm asking to honor my premium pricing. Find your own approach, but have a point of view before you start charging people.

Remember that everything I suggested in this pricing chapter assumes that you are superb and that your work is aligned with your greatest strengths, all of which should support premium pricing. There is also an implicit assumption that you have been doing what you're doing for a while. I don't consider my $95 coffee premium pricing. That was getting-started pricing. If you are receiving adverse feedback ostensibly about your pricing, you may want to take another look at your prices. But you also want to look at the quality and the value of the work you are delivering. In my experience, problems that surface as pricing problems are often quality or delivery problems.

BILL WITH CONFIDENCE

Instead of thinking about billing or invoicing as a purely administrative function, I recommend that you treat billing practices as a part of pricing considerations. You won't regret the extra attention to this issue.

It won't surprise you that I believe in taking a confident stance on billing. When I accept a new piece of work, I am generally titrating my schedule so that I'm available for approximately one less piece of work in the foreseeable future. That is an opportunity cost for me, and I want my new client to put some skin in the game in exchange. Also, I want my client to be fully committed, and one way to commit fully is by issuing payment. Last, and this is a practical consideration, many companies hold invoices for thirty to ninety days as a business practice. This practice can be very hard on small businesses and solopreneurs. So by the time one of my clients pays a first invoice from me, we are often well into the engagement, and I have incurred hard costs like travel in addition to the soft cost of time.

My general practice is to bill for the entirety of the engagement up front. One or two clients have taken issue with this practice. In these cases, I've generally been flexible if I felt confident that I would indeed be paid. But in most cases, my billing practice works without issue, so I can meet my financial obligations and be compensated for the early investments I make in onboarding a new client.

I also have a loosely formulated view on how clients pay me: They will figure it out. I issue the invoice with a brief description of the engagement. If my client needs me to send it to a specific person or use certain language or process it through their procurement system, I do. But it is their responsibility to speak up. Most of my invoices are paid with a bank transfer through my QuickBooks invoices, which includes a small fee. Some are paid by check or through the client's procurement system. On occasion, someone will ask if they can pay with a credit card (who doesn't want those points?). I can do this via QuickBooks, but I rarely say yes and respond that the 3 percent processing fee makes that an unattractive option. If someone hasn't paid or told me payment is on the way in a reasonable amount of time, I follow up with a light touch to ask that they do what they need to do to pay me.

===== **EXERCISE** =====

Parameters for Pricing Yourself

Before you *set* your prices, it is helpful to gain some perspective about what you have earned or need to earn as context for your internal pricing process:

- **Your Current or Most Recent Hourly Rate:** Think about your current job or the last job you held. It may have been hourly, and that makes this easy, but if it was a full-time salaried job, break down your ballpark hourly rate from your salary: divide your approximate monthly gross salary (plus bonus, sales incentives, and the approximate value of your benefits) by the average number of hours you worked per month. This exercise should give you an important data point. This is one example of what you can earn on an hourly basis in the market.

- **Minimum Monthly Budget:** To gain another insight, I recommend that you do a ballpark bare-minimum budget based on a typical month, calculating the core, fixed elements of your life. You may need to use a year for some of these and divide by twelve for averages. For this analysis, you should include at least the following components if applicable. You may have good category summaries from credit-card statements. If you're missing important components, do this exercise over the *next* two months, and track your outlays.

  - » Housing expenses (rent, mortgage, real estate taxes, home insurance)
  - » Home maintenance (yard, cleaning, repairs)
  - » Car payment
  - » Fuel
  - » Student loan payment
  - » Child expenses (care, education, extracurriculars)
  - » Interest on pending credit-card balances
  - » Cable or Internet access
  - » Subscriptions
  - » Cellular phone

» Gym or club membership
» Health insurance premium (if you don't know this because your employer pays now, go on your state exchange and secure a ballpark quote)
» Expected out-of-pocket (deductible) health insurance payments
» Basic travel budget (one or two domestic trips per year)
» Basic food and drink budget (groceries and one to two meals out per week)
» Other things you know you pay monthly or almost monthly (pet expenses, self-care such as haircuts, etc.)

This is your "cost to live." Yes, you can move to a cheaper apartment, but creating a budget for your current life is a good place to start without assuming large life changes. This number, with possible fluctuations to cover good months and bad months, is what you *need* to earn.

These two approaches will help guide you in determining (a) whether what you're trying should be a side hustle or your main thing, (b) whether your work is truly supporting you, and (c) where you should compromise on price based on your ability to make your work work for you.

═══════ **EXERCISE** ═══════
Assessing Your Value as a Building Block for Pricing

Here's a thought experiment about the *value* of what you are or are planning to sell.

+ What is the best way to think about the value you deliver to a prospective client who is your ICP? Is it actual revenue they may generate, a strategic benefit, money or time saved, or something else?
+ Using your selected value methodology, approximately how much value would you be delivering for an engagement based on your ideal scope of work? This will be an estimate. Try to come up with a reasonable dollar value for the sake of this exercise.

+ Take your approximate value estimate and the scope and time commitment being considered and break that down to either an approximate hourly or an approximate monthly income number depending on the example you're using. Compare that finding to your needs from the budget exercise you just completed. How do things line up?
+ You may price yourself below your value. That's fine. In my experience, knowing your value will help you price in a healthier way and quiet your imposter voice if she happens to get verbose.
+ As a gut check, you may wish to compare the price you land on to what you believe others at your level might charge in the market. Because I think perfect comparisons are difficult to make and because I prefer using value and earnings goals as my primary pricing methodologies, I don't worry much about the market in setting a price. That said, I sometimes think about comparisons in *talking about my price to a prospect*. If I am at what I think is the top of the market, I might mention this to qualify a prospect, conserve time if I may be outside a prospect's budget, or engage in a referral conversation.

EXERCISE
Pairing Your Scope and Pricing

+ Identify three different scopes of work you can publish as standard offerings. Even if you do custom work, do this as an exercise to test your views on pricing.
+ For each scope, think about your floor price and your target price. Consider the goals you set earlier in this book and any market research or pricing discussions you have had.
+ Then, for each offering, list two objections to your price target that a prospect might have. Some of these objections may be generic: "The market is flat" or "I'm facing a ton of budget pressure at year end." And some may be specific to you: "I've never seen a number like this for what you do" or "Your imputed rates

couldn't possibly generate the ROI we would need to reach for this to make sense."

- Craft two arguments you would use to address those objections. Remember in your arguments to account for passionate ambivalence. Also remember that, in some of those objection scenarios, you may simply agree; if the ROI of what you plan to do in a specific situation doesn't warrant a rate that you believe in, that prospect may not be a good fit for what you do, or it might be wise to change your price. That's okay, and it's good to know early in a pricing discussion.

CHAPTER 24

GETTING TO A CLOSE

You've optimized your marketing funnel. The flywheel is working. You've massaged highly qualified leads so that they became "fit calls." You conferred about pricing. Neither you nor your prospect has politely declined. Now it's time to close the deal. Here are four primary scenarios:

1. You close on the phone.
2. You send an email with some follow-up and get to yes via a reply.
3. You don't hear from the prospect, and they reach out six months later to do the work you previously discussed.
4. You never hear from your prospect again.

Let's dig into recommendations on how to handle each of these scenarios.

1. YOU CLOSE ON THE PHONE

In this scenario, your fit call goes great. You share a common vision about what work should happen, how it should happen, and what it should cost. Your prospect says, "Let's go."

You may be thinking that this scenario never happens. In my experience, it happens all the time. One reason some people think it doesn't happen is that they are unwilling to allow themselves to believe it happens. So when it does start to happen, they interfere. Instead, let it happen.

It's critical to listen on a fit or follow-up call for all the signals—what the client wants, what concerns they have, timing, fears, hopes, and green lights. When you get a green light, you want to notice it and solidify it on the call. You want to reply with something like "Fantastic! I really look forward to working with you and your team." You do not want to say something like "Well, before you say yes, let me get you a full proposal and a draft contract."

Not listening for green lights can be an upper-limit behavior. Notice that. Take a deep breath and welcome the yes.

When I get a fit call green light, I let the prospect know on the call what will happen next:

> I have two meetings this afternoon, but I will get you an email summarizing our plan by 5 p.m. today. When I send that email, I will also send you an invoice for the engagement and my firm's W-9 for your finance team. I will also send you a kickoff email outlining next steps and requesting materials and meeting dates from you for our engagement.

After I say that or something like it, I do those things. When I send those follow-up communications, nothing contained in them includes any sense that we have not closed on this partnership. We're going. The train has left the station. It's no longer about whether but about how. Details. This tone is critical for tenderly holding the close you just secured and ensuring that everyone is moving forward. This tone is clear and declarative, which at this point is wholly consistent with passionate ambivalence.

2. YOU SEND AN EMAIL WITH SOME FOLLOW-UP AND GET TO "YES"

Sometimes a fit call ends and the close hasn't happened. I often engineer this result in service of passionate ambivalence. I might say something like

"Well, this is exciting, but why don't you sleep on it, and if you're game to move forward after that, let me know and we'll make it happen." Why do I say that? I want to ensure that they feel that they have space. I don't want to feel like I'm overselling.

Sometimes the delay is at the request of the prospect. This might sound something like "Well, I need to run this by the others on my team. Can you get me a proposal summarizing what we just discussed with all the details clearly outlined?" When I get this request, I'm delighted to do it if it feels clear to me (in my gut) that this isn't a delaying tactic—that it's a genuine desire to see and share a clear summary of what we've been discussing. When I get this request, I will typically say exactly this:

Sure. I'll be happy to send you a summary of what I've proposed. I want to let you know, however, that it won't come in the form of a prepackaged sixteen-page proposal. I don't do that. What I'm going to send you is a concise summary of our discussion, my proposed scope of work, and key financial considerations in a set of emailed bullet points. You have likely experienced me as direct and concise, and I'll do it this way to conserve time for both of us.

When I say this, I'm serving a few goals. First, I don't want to write a lengthy prose proposal. Second, I want to share a concise sense of what is in front of us so my prospect (and perhaps the decision-maker above her) can act quickly. Third, this is my style, and I am endeavoring to show up as me in every stage of the sales process.

Now, when I send a bullet-list "proposal" by email, an act I've done hundreds of times, I *take pains to show* that I have listened diligently to what my prospect said in our conversations. I reiterate the ways I am a perfect option for their needs. I sell with passionate ambivalence. My last line of that email will say something like "Let me know when you want to move forward." It will *definitely not say* "Let me know if you have questions." I write this kind of note as a presumptive sale. I'll field any questions from them as they assimilate my email, but I will narrow the path to close in my communications to them. I may even convey some sense of urgency or scarcity if that feels authentic and not manipulative.

My half-page proposal email often generates back-and-forth, which is great. It may generate just a "Let's do this," in which case I move to scenario 1 and follow those steps. It also may generate crickets.

If it does generate crickets, I will probably not follow up. I hold this belief lightly. I'm not sure I'm right. But sometimes passionate ambivalence makes me do (er, not do) things like this. The most I would ever do in this situation is send a single note to my prospect that forwards my previous email and says, "I wanted to be sure this reached you, and regardless of your decision, it was terrific to get to know you and your company in this process." That's it.

3. YOU DON'T HEAR FROM THE PROSPECT, AND THEY REACH OUT SIX MONTHS LATER TO DO THE WORK YOU PREVIOUSLY DISCUSSED

Terrific. Follow the aforementioned scenario 1 or 2 and do a happy dance if you're still available and game to do the work.

4. YOU NEVER HEAR FROM YOUR PROSPECT AGAIN

Ah, well, you'll get 'em next time.

I am sure some people will do postmortems on losing a sale like this. That's a perfectly reasonable thing to do; it's just not something I do. There are many factors in a sales decision, many of which have nothing to do with me, you, or anything that happened in the process. I also don't ask for feedback on what didn't fit. I've come to think after decades of terminating employees and saying no to investment opportunities that it is quite rare to receive feedback on the actual reason a negative thing happened. Instead, I direct my attention to the next opportunity and assume that the fit just wasn't there for one reason or another.

It is in these precious situations that I tune into the "ambivalent" side of passionate ambivalence.

LISTEN FOR SIGNALS

Before leaving the topic of closing, I want to remind you of my earlier admonition to listen for signals that it would be wise for you to politely decline a piece of work. I've felt since my early lawyer days that you learn more about another party during negotiations than at any other time in a relationship. Pay attention. Listen for signs that your trust isn't warranted. Listen for any signs that don't feel aligned with your top two core values or your sense of well-being. And if you hear those signals, politely decline. It doesn't matter how far down the road you are. Better to step away at the altar than to have an unhappy business marriage.

DON'T JUST DO THE WORK—LOVE THE WORK

There is one more thing I pay attention to at this moment in the sales cycle and at most previous stages. The entire thread about whether I want the work, like the prospect, feel good about the pricing, and think that the scope of the project aligns with my zone of genius is all about ensuring that when I do get to close, the engagement is a great success. I and surely you will always *do the work*, but my goal is loftier than that. I want to *love* the work and develop genuine respect if not admiration for my client. I want to be vested in the success of my individual or company clients. Remember that all my goals I shared in Chapter 12 roll up to joy and freedom. The way this special alchemy surfaces at the closing stage for me is that once I start doing the work, I generally aspire to *overdeliver* on my commitments to my client, to exceed expectations.

I look for opportunities to be even more valuable than they thought I would be. I am an advocate for my client in the market in ways they don't expect. I have no issue taking phone calls on a Sunday while I'm waiting in line at Disney World (this is not a hypothetical example) because a client wants to discuss something urgent. I will do a call or two with a challenging team member whom my client manages even though we didn't agree to that at the start. I will facilitate a complex conversation with an individual client and their spouse or do a mentoring call with a client's kid. I aim to be a client's "unfair advantage" by virtue of being exemplary. I don't do all that because I *have to*. I do it because I *want to*. One of the great benefits of passionate ambivalence is it engenders genuine commitment at the end of a sales process and throughout a working relationship. And overdelivering, as much as or more than anything else I've discussed in this book, keeps the sales flywheel of my business moving. But in truth, I overdeliver for the fun and satisfaction, not for the flywheel.

ACCEPTING FEEDBACK

Whether or not your business or selling effort is progressing toward your goals, it's critical to routinely expose yourself to feedback from your clients on the quality of your work and your impact. Feedback will make you better at how you sell and what you do. As such, you should seek feedback from clients and prospects, especially when you spend a good chunk of time selling something and then receive an unexpected late-in-the-game no.

I want to pause here to acknowledge that feedback isn't always pleasant to receive. I am an avid seeker of and advocate for feedback, but I often notice a tightness in my gut when someone asks if I'm open to feedback. My subconscious recoils: *Ouch! Really? Aren't I perfect?* I usually get the feedback. Then I take a breath and check whether defensiveness is arising in me. I take another breath and express appreciation for what I've just learned. Even if I don't agree in the moment, I usually reflect on feedback later. I try not to beat myself up about it. And I often find at least one nugget of value in what someone has shared. Like any good exercise regimen, soliciting, hearing, and processing feedback takes practice, but developing those muscles is important for ongoing self-reflection and growth. It is important to remember that feedback can be positive or negative. You want to attend to both types so you have better insight on whether to continue doing something the way you have been or whether to shift. The benefits to you and your business will be meaningful.

Here are a few recommended practices for garnering and leveraging feedback to amplify your sales success, grow your business, and lean even more into your zone of genius at work.

Tune Your Feedback Monitor

If you think feedback is surgical, that it happens only in official feedback sessions, annual reviews, or postmortems on a project, you are missing out on a ton of quality feedback. I recommend that you tune your feedback monitor to a more sensitive setting and pay attention to the informal signals that are happening all around you during a sales process or the delivery of whatever it is you recently sold.

Here are a few examples of things that might constitute relevant feedback:

+ You quote a price for a piece of work and get an immediate yes. That might be a signal that your pricing is right or that it is on the low side.
+ Your prospect or client has canceled a few meetings at the last minute. This might be an indication that the sales effort or project isn't going well.
+ During status updates on a project over Zoom, you notice that your client seems to be multitasking, going on and off video. Perhaps whatever you are sharing or how you are sharing it isn't as compelling as it could be.
+ You're working with a team, and the most senior team member stops attending your meetings. If your buyer is a senior leader, you may want to find out what is behind their absences.
+ You conducted a workshop for a customer, and one of their colleagues reaches out to see if you could also do a workshop for their team. Positive feedback! Have a fit call. Draft an invoice!

I am not recommending that you make yourself nuts by over-relying on passive feedback signs. I simply suggest that you pay attention, particularly when the words you *are* hearing from a prospect or a customer do not align with your internal sense of how things are going.

Ask and Ask Again

You should be asking explicitly and often for feedback. Consider a question like "How did you feel about this conversation?" at the end of a fit call or in an email follow-up. If you are working with a client, create routine opportunities during an engagement to use a check-in call or a more formal feedback survey to see how you're doing. Ask your customer what they want you to start doing, continue doing, and stop doing. It's a simple structure and usually requires a light lift from your customer. Ensure that you convey that you're not fishing for compliments but interested in concrete corrective or reinforcing feedback to strengthen your partnership.

If you are asking for feedback but not receiving anything useful, the feedback may be too general to be actionable. Perhaps the feedback seems to be coming from someone who would prefer to avoid conflict. If you notice that you're not getting the meat of the input, do your best to give the other party even more permission to be honest with you in service of working together even more effectively. Ask for details or examples.

It is worth noting that you should feel free to ask for feedback during or after an engagement, but you also might ask for it after a fit call that didn't lead to business you wanted. You may or may not gain useful insight in this scenario, but asking gives you the chance to learn and may enhance the way your prospect perceives you.

Give Feedback Yourself

I find that one of the fastest ways to get more feedback is to give more feedback. Giving feedback is often as vulnerable as receiving it, so your willingness to share constructive feedback might instill a greater sense of trust with a client and produce more mutual feedback. Tell your customer that their multitasking is distracting. Remind them that last-minute cancellations are disruptive. Praise their ability to be prompt and clear.

Receive Feedback Like a Pro

When someone gives you honest, direct feedback, it will generally be most difficult to accept when you consciously or unconsciously believe it contains a grain of truth. This means that you are *most likely to be resistant* to the most valuable and truthful feedback. The stakes are highest in the most challenging situations.

The most common amateur move in response to feedback is defensiveness, which includes classic defensiveness ("That's not what happened at all!") and more passive defensiveness ("Let me just explain to you *why* I did it that way!"). As I mentioned, giving honest feedback is vulnerable and, at a minimum, time-consuming. If you reward it with a brick wall or worse, you will miss out on the best way to make yourself a more effective human and self-aware seller.

If you want to receive feedback like a pro, whether you've asked for it or not, here are my recommendations:

+ Take a breath and calm your nervous system.
+ Listen. Really listen. Or read if the feedback is written.
+ Pay attention to whether your brain is screaming all sorts of reasons the person is wrong. If that is happening, and it will often happen, keep breathing and return to listening or reading.
+ Consider paraphrasing or repeating what your feedback provider just said: "I heard you say that I interrupted you multiple times in that last meeting."
+ Express gratitude for the feedback by saying "Thank you," and let the person know that you would like to think about what you've heard and circle back to them (if that's true) in a few hours or a few days.

I strongly recommend against replying in the moment. If you reply in the moment, you will almost *certainly* be defensive. You will miss the value of the feedback. You will compromise trust with the feedback provider. You will seem closed and self-righteous. You will be in a feedback arms race by, possibly, offering your side of the situation. All these options are not in your long-term interest, so avoid them. Thank the feedback provider and offer a future action plan.

HOW IS IT TRUE?

Once you've received a bit of constructive feedback and you've followed the aforementioned steps, you most likely will think of all the reasons and ways what that other person just told you is wrong. Human nature. Fair enough. Happily, you will only be thinking these thoughts while taking a walk, taking deep breaths, or playing with your dog (dogs give the best feedback!).

Once you get past those minutes or hours of intensity, I suggest that you ask yourself a question I learned from spiritual leader Byron Katie in her book *Loving What Is*. Instead of asking, "How is what I heard wrong?" ask yourself, "How is what I heard true?" Even if you come up with only one or two tiny ways in which it's true, the exercise will make you more open to the feedback you received.

After you've found more openness, you can do a couple things. First, you can circle back to the person who gave you feedback and have an open, honest conversation in service of mutual learning. Second, you can pick and choose what you might want to change about your thinking or approach based on the feedback you received. Absent a customer or a boss telling you that you must change a thing they don't like, you have a choice about what parts of any feedback you take or leave. Frankly, you have options even if a customer or boss tells you that you must make a change.

═══════════════ **EXERCISE** ═══════════════
Noticing Passive Feedback Signals

+ Think about your work over the last three months. Look at emails related to that work, and think of past conversations or meetings. Consider the momentum of your selling efforts.
+ What types of passive, unintentional feedback have you received from your prospects or customers? Be honest with yourself without being too harsh.
+ What one or two actions could you take to address the perceived informal feedback you have received, including perhaps asking for explicit feedback (see the following exercises)?

====== **EXERCISE** ======

Increasing the Frequency of Feedback During an Engagement

I often request feedback during an engagement to ensure that I am on track with a client on a piece of work. I encourage you to do this, too, especially after milestones in the engagement. If you are currently involved with any customer, try this exercise right now.

- Ask your key customer stakeholders how things are going in your engagement. Are they satisfied with your work to date? Are there things you should start, continue, or stop doing?
- If you gain valuable insight from this feedback, follow up with a message sharing what you plan to change in response.

====== **EXERCISE** ======

Increasing the Quality of Feedback After an Engagement

- If you have a feedback mechanism (e.g., a survey) that you use after you work with clients, look at the quality of the feedback you have received in the last three uses.
- If you received specific, constructive feedback, ask yourself whether you have acted on one or two of the specific insights you received.
- If you do not feel that you have been receiving *any* deep and specific corrective feedback, come up with one to three new questions (or new ways of asking old questions) to increase the quality and specificity of the responses. Consider additions such as
  - » "Give me one example of something you felt I could have done better."
  - » "Specifically, what did you see in my approach that was less than superb?"
  - » "What could I have done differently?"

- If you use a digital survey, make questions about areas for improvement mandatory, not optional. Give contextually relevant examples of discerning feedback as guidelines for what you might expect in tone and depth.

- If you do not have a survey, create one now on any platform you like (Google Forms is fine and free). Then send it to a client after your next engagement or first meeting or two.

CHAPTER 25

HOW THINGS EVOLVE

Jelling, Failing, Exploding

For many solopreneurs, particularly those who are working through the exercises in this book, things will slowly start to jell. And then the momentum will increase. The more superb work you do, the more work you will have the chance to do. People are always looking for excellence, and people *love to talk to other people* when they are experiencing excellence. Your flywheel will begin to turn.

When that happens, pause to notice and celebrate it. When you get *your call* that you cannot believe in a Target, when you get a referral who mentions they heard about you from someone you don't even know, when you receive three qualified inquiries on your site in one week, do a happy dance! This is extraordinary. It's a result of the great work you've done within yourself, on your sales funnel, and with your clients. Way to go! Be sure you have one or two people in your world who will welcome you to brag, brag, and brag. Take every chance you can, within yourself and with your most trusted people, to mark your milestones in a way that matters. Then—

INCREASE YOUR FOCUS

Double down. Notice where the momentum is happening in your work. What kinds of prospects are reaching out most? What parts of your offerings are drawing the most enthusiasm from prospects and clients? This moment in your business is proof that you've reached the often elusive product-market fit. When you get there, increase your focus on those areas or those prospect and client types to take advantage of the energy flowing in your direction. Start new offerings in *these* areas that might scale or generate more revenue per unit of work. Pitch new people in these client categories by leveraging your network. Tweak your bio or your site to amplify these areas. Add testimonials from satisfied customers.

The only reason *not* to do this is if the areas that are resonating most strongly with prospects and clients are not resonating well with you. That might happen, but it's unlikely. Most people gravitate to people who are working in their zone of genius. So these spots of growth and momentum are likely right in your wheelhouse.

There is one general human tendency I have seen play out in this situation that isn't terribly useful. In my experience, entrepreneurs (and many others) find it challenging to let go of anything they are doing, especially if it is driving *some* success. They make up a story that they "need to do it all" to please prospects and keep growing. If you have this thought, I encourage you to consider the upside you may experience in a few weeks or months by narrowing your focus to what is working best (and is in your zone of genius). Any temporary revenue setback should result in an eventual expansion of the business you love the most with clients you value at prices you seek.

BEWARE UPPER-LIMIT THOUGHTS

When things start to jell, when you have more incoming demand than you can or want to engage, you get to do all sorts of extremely fun things. You will likely have an opportunity to increase your prices based on this new demand. Try it. It might feel scary. You might have the thought that if you get more expensive, you will close fewer deals and lose your momentum. These are upper-limit thoughts, and if you've been paying attention, there is at least as much chance that raising your prices will *increase the demand for your work*. That shows you the power of passionate ambivalence. Also, even if you close fewer deals, you might be generating more total revenue. Less work. More revenue. Good equation.

Additionally, this might be an opportunity to start looking around your network for a referral partner to whom you can send business you cannot handle. That's when the magic really begins. In addition to generating active income by doing the work you're hired to do, you obtain passive income from referral sources. You also might get a lot of love from those referral partners and a chance to pay back the karma of incoming referrals in your early days.

Don't let unconscious commitments or upper-limit thoughts hold you back in this moment of jelling. Lean in. Grow. Flow. Flourish. Dance. There are never enough reminders to dance.

WHAT IF THIS STRATEGY IS "FAILING"?

I warned you early on, but I want to reiterate it here. This strategy of selling with a focus on your gifts and a mindset of passionate ambivalence will fail regularly. By "fail," I mean that you will lose prospective sales that you really wanted. You will feel great after a fit call, and you will start mentally considering that chunk of revenue part of your successful move toward your annual goal. And then you will hear nothing, or you will hear that your prospect chose someone else. I lose sales, too, occasionally as a direct result of the strategies I've shared in this book. If I were flexible in my pricing, if I were slightly more deferential in an occasional prospect fit call, if I routinely *asked* for the sale, I would probably pick up a few extra sales a year.

If you are like me, you will also lose clients you hoped would engage with you over a longer time horizon. Passionate ambivalence does not prevent me from feeling bad about this and from looking back over my actions with a client to see what I did "wrong." Sometimes I beat myself up for a day or two, and some losses last a bit longer. Eventually, I return to equanimity about this, pick up the lesson I obtained (after the beating-myself-up part, which is not extremely useful in terms of personal growth), and move on to what I assume will be as or more interesting work in my future.

FIND YOUR AUTHENTIC VERSION
OF PASSIONATE AMBIVALENCE

If you look at things on a daily or weekly basis, you will run into prospects who think passionate ambivalence is neutral at best and obnoxious at worst. This is why it is *critical* that you find *your authentic* version of passionate ambivalence. You will still lose sales if you're authentic, but when I show up exactly as myself in sales conversations, I don't have many regrets when I lose something. When I show up in persona, as something other than myself, I do have regrets when things don't fly. I endeavor to avoid that, and I've endeavored to provide you with a wide range of tools to help you avoid it, too.

When you look at your sales progress over months and years, I believe these strategies will pay off in the long run. You will be more likely to achieve your financial and personal goals. You will connect with work and people you love at price points that feel aligned with your sense of your own value. That's a winning combination.

WHAT IF PASSIONATE AMBIVALENCE DOESN'T WORK?

If you try these tactics and they don't work, I encourage you to look inside yourself. Go back to the early chapters and evaluate whether you've followed the guidelines of selling yourself as yourself. If you have done all this internal work and external research on your sector and your offering, it may be time to pivot. Look at your results and see how you are presenting yourself, how you are marketing, how your fit calls are going, and how you are presenting or delivering a product or service that is or isn't resonating with the market based on the explicit and implicit feedback you're receiving. Receiving your lessons from small or large failures is essential to building an ever-stronger operation. This active learning-and-iterating cycle is not for the faint of heart. It takes pure openness to where you may be off in your efforts followed by tenacity in making changes, trying new experiments, and finding what works for you in your market.

Two years ago, I did the first of what turned out to be many sessions with a Young Presidents' Organization forum in San Francisco. Yong Kim,

CEO (chief empathy officer) of Wonolo, was one of the participants in this small group. At the end of the session, I asked the group members to email any feedback for me. Yong sent a detailed email. Some of his observations were positive; some were negative. I keep the entire full-page email pasted in my running to-do list in Asana under the title "Read this before any gig!" I read this before any gig because Yong pointed to a few places where I know I have screwed up when I've been caught up in the intensity of the moment with a person or a group. To show you how badly I can fail and still be hired again by the same group (and sometimes when I screw up, I am not rehired, and that's okay), I thought I'd share his most astute and most searing (to me) feedback:

> I did not appreciate how Sue gave feedback to each person at the end. I felt that some comments were uncalled for, judgmental, and unactionable. For example, she used the word "boring" to Mara. It was unclear whether Sue was just expressing her story in her head or giving actual feedback that each person could work on. If feedback is not actionable, is that feedback? I was so confused about what Sue did. It did not land to me like feedback, and I wish she could have ended each observation with something actionable that each person could work on.

Have I used that facilitation exercise since? No. I have not. I have pivoted. And if I ever get close to forgetting how far I got from quality work at that moment on that day, I have Yong's feedback front and center.

A BIGGER PIVOT

If the market is not responding on your desired or needed timeline despite your flexing to meet clients' needs and tweaking messaging and pricing to meet prospects where they are (under the assumption that something in your approach may be off), it may be time to pivot in a bigger way. You can pivot in the work you provide, or you can get a job. Everything you've read in this book will help you in any traditional job, whether you are a financial analyst at a Fortune 500 company or an account executive at a software startup.

You also do not have to treat this as *one decision*. Side hustles are the new black. If you want to try your hand at doing something on your own, give it a shot while maintaining your day job. This was the choice I made in 1999 when I wanted to give the Internet a whirl without the risk of losing my home to the bank. This is a logical choice to make, and absent a specific clause in any document you have with your employer that prohibits you from making it, you might be able to find the time. Kicking things off as a side hustle gives you a chance to see if you like working on your own. Just as important, it may allow you to solidify customer relationships before making the jump to your own full-time company. This is a massive advantage, proof that you and whatever you're up to have a credible, valuable business offering or product-market fit. That's gold.

I want you to be happy. I want you to be safe. If this recipe isn't working, I trust you'll make the choices that support your own flourishing in a different way. As I said, I've made major shifts in my career, from law to tech to coaching. I regret none of them. Due to the breadth of my experience, I have tremendous range. If you've run a business that focuses primarily on you, you've tried something extraordinary. If the experiment works, that's super. If the experiment doesn't deliver, take your ball of knowledge and keep trying to find the magical alignment that makes your heart (and bank account) sing.

EXERCISE
Is It Time to Pivot?

Here's a thought experiment if you find yourself concerned that things aren't working for you in the way (or close to the way) I've shared in this book.

+ Revisit the goals you set in Chapter 12. Let's assume you have twelve months to hit some of the key elements of those goals. Depending on where you are in your selling journey, honestly evaluate how you are doing. Remember, the first six months may go more slowly than the second six months. But give this a candid review.

+ Revisit the cost-to-live budget you set in Chapter 23. How is it going? Are you struggling to pay bills? Have you exhausted your nonretirement savings? Are you dipping into your retirement savings and paying a penalty on distributions? How much longer can you make this work? What kind of feedback are you receiving from your life partner or close friends about your progress on the financial front?

+ Open LinkedIn or your job board of choice and look at the other options you might have if you decide to get a more traditional job. Look at those salary ranges and compare them to what you are bringing in now and what is on the expected horizon. Remember to build in the expenses of health insurance and other benefits that may be covered by a full-time employer.

+ If you're not ready, based on this review, to try something different, set a date three months hence to do this exercise again. In this moment, set expectations to which you will hold yourself on that future date. Ask a friend or partner to hold you accountable to this future review.

IF THINGS EXPLODE AND "YOU" GET BIGGER THAN YOU

In rare and beautiful moments, companies that are launched with a primary dependency on the founder will become bigger than anyone ever imagined. This may not have been the plan, but when the jelling continues to jell; when the referral network is so large that it makes sense to hire additional employees; or when the product, service, or idea gains so much steam that any dependency on the founder now feels parochial, something very interesting has happened. I'm not suggesting that this is better, but I am pointing out that it happens so that you can notice these signs in your own business and make good choices from there.

Vlada Bortnik, Cofounder and CEO, Marco Polo

When Vlada Bortnik speaks about Marco Polo in public, people want to use the company's video chat app more. She is the embodiment of the philosophy of selling from the starting point of herself and of selling without attachment to whether her prospective customers buy.

Vlada and her husband, Michal, founded Marco Polo in 2012. They were about to have their first child and wanted to model a good life for her. Vlada thought, *Okay, we're going to spend this big chunk of our day working; let's make sure we're doing something that's personally meaningful and something that would make a big difference in the world*. Then they went big: They decided to do something that would produce more happiness in the world. "Both of us can be pretty audacious in terms of what we think we can do," says Vlada. "We immersed ourselves in happiness research." The key to happiness? Close relationships.

Vlada and Michal both have family overseas. They didn't feel that social media, Skype, and texting were really tapping the magic of technology to eliminate the sense of being out of touch with loved ones.

At first, Vlada and Michal didn't know what their company would do. But they decided to raise money in support of their vision that technology could help bolster connection. They intended to run several experiments to find the right solution, so they knew they needed patient investors who also believed in the vision. And investors responded very well, again and again.

Even though Vlada was successful at raising money, she was resistant to putting herself at the heart of her pitch. "I don't know if it's partially about being female, but I didn't really want the spotlight," she says. In 2019, she and a colleague were on a business trip, and in one of their meetings, the colleague pressed Vlada to tell the founder story for five minutes. "I literally rolled my eyes but agreed," says Vlada. "There were thirty people in the room, and the impact of my story was palpable. That was the moment I understood that I needed to put myself in the story of Marco Polo." Vlada now speaks publicly more often, and she uses LinkedIn and other platforms to express her vision.

Marco Polo does extensive research on how its app affects feelings of connection and loneliness. After launching a paid version of the product midway through the company's journey, Marco Polo discovered that once users knew the company's founding story, their likelihood of upgrading to the paid version increased by 30 percent.

"I have heard that something about me makes a difference," says Vlada. "But I honestly think it's just knowing that we're not a heartless tech company." Marco Polo doesn't sell user data. It has made public commitments to protect privacy. It ensures that its audience is aware of these commitments.

Vlada and Michal continue to be intentional about living their lives with purpose. "When we started the company," Vlada says, "we thought the biggest risk was that at some point, we wouldn't want to work on it. And so every year on our wedding anniversary, we take a few days away from everybody, and we ask how we're doing. It still feels wonderful. I am more energized now than I was before. And in our years of work on the project, the need has only grown more significant."

WILL PASSIONATE AMBIVALENCE WORK IF EVERYONE KNOWS YOU'RE DOING IT?

My own business exploded to the point where I have distilled my learning into this book. At various points in its writing, I read portions aloud to my husband, Eliot, starting with the very first, very shitty draft. One day, after I shared the chapter on fit calls, a phase where passionate ambivalence really shines, Eliot asked me, "What effect do you think this book is going to have on your future ability to sell?" For example, when I tell a prospect, as I sometimes do, that I have limited time in the fall season and would like a commitment, will they believe me?

Gulp. In truth, I hadn't given that a second thought.

But here we are. It's one thing for me to risk my business by publishing my commitment to selling through passionate ambivalence. It's another thing to leave you, fair reader, wondering whether the very existence of this book and the dissemination of this strategy will render it impotent. Even worse, you're getting notice of this concern in the last two pages!

Take heart. My answer for both of us is passionate, emphatic, and not at all ambivalent.

I don't see passionate ambivalence as a parlor trick or a ruse. Instead, everything I have shared here is an honest articulation of what I have seen drive sales success over the course of different careers and contexts. Moreover, my selling methodology requires that you develop a highly attuned sense of yourself, that you put yourself out there in ways that are superb and helpful, that you price yourself in accordance with your value, that you stand for doing phenomenal work at price points that are supported by your customers' ROI, and that you keep your head up and stay unattached to whether you win or lose any particular sale.

Every component of this approach requires you to be in the business of building trust by showing up authentically and delivering or overdelivering on your commitments. From that position, you will be able to get the next sale if you don't get this one. You will create a flywheel that leads you to great work with your treasured customers and clients. You will most likely be busy this fall, even if you're not that busy the first time someone asks you about it.

This book is an invitation for you to become more, not less, honest—with yourself and with your prospects. If you followed along and completed the exercises here in earnest, you won't need to act passionately ambivalent. You will *be* passionately ambivalent. It's perfectly fine if you and your prospects know that about you. Frankly, it should make you even more attractive as a business partner. That's the point.

ACKNOWLEDGMENTS

I would be nowhere on the journey that forms the basis of this book without my current and former clients and program participants. At some point or points, you said "yes" to something I was offering. I hope I have represented that experience and you well. Most of what I've learned in the last decade I've learned from you.

Leah Pearlman, mentioned so often in this text, helped identify this topic as "my book." Then she provided a first generous and discerning read. Evan Hung, Heather Frick, Kim Wagner, and Tina Scala were also on that couch on the night we decided I would run the sales-focused workshop that formed the basis for this book.

Many people identified in this book graciously agreed to be interviewed or to review and approve my reflections about them for inclusion here. Thank you for being so formative in my thinking.

I also garnered lessons from the following folks who were not explicitly mentioned: Barry Schwartz, Ronnie Schwartz, Shannah Van Winkle, Mark Leffers, Cameron Henneke, Harish Venkatesan, Andrew Ledet, and Dave Mayer.

Kimberly Weisul was a crack editor of early drafts, offering her superb insights on the story arc in concert with her strong understanding of business. Natalie Lampert helped me crystallize my message and the voices of many sidebar stories.

I received invaluable feedback and support from early readers Danielle Dannenberg, Natty Zola, Scott Peppet, Brad Bernthal, and Charlie Besecker.

Bettina Elias Siegel, Justin Evans, Jerry Colonna, and Nate Klemp all helped me in meaningful ways to navigate the process of securing a literary agent and selling a manuscript to a publisher. My entrepreneurial literary agent, Michael Signorelli, co-created and executed a plan to sell this book using the very practices espoused in it. Dan Ambrosio made a bet on me and gave this book its title. Renee Sedliar, my editor, pushed me to make this book more relevant to more people. She offered a number of reflections I valued for this book and for myself. And she eradicated any story I ever had that the publishing business moves slowly. Renee is fast! Thanks to Sean Moreau and Emily Baker for assistance in production, Connie Oehring for copyediting, Susan VanHecke and Cindy Black for proofreading, Julie Hodgins for image design, Jeff Stiefel for layout design, Jim Datz for cover design, and Alexandra Hernandez and Laura Gonzalez for marketing and PR.

Thanks to my teachers and collaborators in the work of conscious leadership: Kaley Klemp, Jim Dethmer, Diana Chapman, and Grace Clayton. Thanks also to the formative insights of Gay Hendricks and Byron Katie.

My executive business partner and friend, Liz Nelson, graces me with her collaboration. She is the single greatest contributor to the success of my solopreneur business. She touches everything, and everything is far better by virtue of her touch.

I would never have the life I have if it weren't for three people who pay attention to and support me in my zone of genius: Leah Pearlman; my brother, Mike Heilbronner; and my partner, Eliot Ephraim. When I finally decided to really write a book, these three people reminded me again and again that I might have something useful to say.

Thanks to Brad Feld, who said yes to an investment in the MergeLane Fund in minutes and again said yes to writing the foreword to this book on a similar timeline.

Thanks finally to my adopted hometown of Boulder, Colorado, and to the extraordinary and collegial #givefirst culture that has spurred me and so many wonderful people to chase their dreams and support the dreams of others.

INDEX

ABOUT THE AUTHOR

SUE HEILBRONNER has been an operator, lawyer, venture capitalist, professor, and executive coach with a primary focus on tech since the dawn of the consumer Internet. She has worked with executives and teams from companies like Google, Meta, Apple, G2, Guild, Salesforce, and more. Culture Amp has named her one of the top twenty-two executive coaches in the world. Sue is the cofounder of MergeLane, a venture capital fund focused on companies with at least one woman in leadership. She also co-created the Certification for Leader Coaches, which offers coaching certifications to leaders who wish to integrate more coaching tools and mindsets into their day-to-day jobs. Sue is an active blogger on the intersection of business and conscious leadership at www.heysue.com and the host of the *HeySue* podcast, which offers live coaching to business guests.

RAISING READERS
Books Build Bright Futures

Thank you for reading this book and for being a reader of books in general. As a author, I am so grateful to share being part of a community of readers with you and I hope you will join me in passing our love of books on to the next generatio of readers.

Did you know that reading for enjoyment is the single biggest predictor of child's future happiness and success?

More than family circumstances, parents' educational background, or income reading impacts a child's future academic performance, emotional well-being communication skills, economic security, ambition, and happiness.

Studies show that kids reading for enjoyment in the US is in rapid decline:

- In 2012, 53% of 9-year-olds read almost every day. Just 10 years later, in 2022, the number had fallen to 39%.
- In 2012, 27% of 13-year-olds read for fun daily. By 2023, that number was just 14%.

Together, we can commit to **Raising Readers** and change this trend. How?

- Read to children in your life daily.
- Model reading as a fun activity.
- Reduce screen time.
- Start a family, school, or community book club.
- Visit bookstores and libraries regularly.
- Listen to audiobooks.
- Read the book before you see the movie.
- Encourage your child to read aloud to a pet or stuffed animal.
- Give books as gifts.
- Donate books to families and communities in need.

BOB1217

Books build bright futures, and **Raising Readers** is our shared responsibility.

For more information, visit **JoinRaisingReaders.com**

Sources: National Endowment for the Arts, National Assessment of Educational Progress. WorldBookDay.org, Nielsen BookData's 2023 "Understanding the Children's Book Consumer"